The New Media Epidemic

THE
NEW MEDIA
EPIDEMIC

THE UNDERMINING OF SOCIETY, FAMILY, AND OUR OWN SOUL

Jean-Claude Larchet
Translated by Archibald Andrew Torrance

HOLY TRINITY PUBLICATIONS
The Printshop of St Job of Pochaev
Holy Trinity Monastery
Jordanville, New York

Printed with the blessing of His Eminence,
Metropolitan Hilarion First Hierarch
of the Russian Orthodox Church Outside of Russia

The New Media Epidemic © 2019 Holy Trinity Monastery

PRINTSHOP OF
SAINT JOB OF POCHAEV

An imprint of

HOLY TRINITY PUBLICATIONS
Holy Trinity Monastery
Jordanville, New York 13361-0036
www.holytrinitypublications.com

Cover Design: James Bozeman
Cover Art: *Social Media Seamless Background* by bubaone,
180326853m, gettyimages.com.

Originally published in French: Jean-Claude Larchet., Malade des
nouveaux médias (Paris, France: Éditions du Cerf, 2016) 978-2204114868.

ISBN: 978-0-88465-471-1 (paperback)
ISBN: 978-0-88465-427-8 (ePub)
ISBN: 978-0-88465-428-5 (Mobipocket)

Library of Congress Control Number 2018961551

Quotes from THE SHALLOWS: WHAT THE INTERNET IS
DOING TO OUR BRAINS by Nicholas Carr. Copyright © 2010 by
Nicholas Carr. Used by permission of W. W. Norton & Company, Inc.

New Testament Scripture passages taken from the New King James Version.
Copyright © 1982 by Thomas Nelson, Inc. Used by permission.
Psalms taken from A Psalter for Prayer, trans. David James
(Jordanville, N.Y.: Holy Trinity Publications, 2011).
Old Testament and Deuterocanonical passages taken
from the Orthodox Study Bible. Copyright © 2008 by Thomas Nelson,
Inc. Used by permission.

Contents

Addicts of Modern Media

For death has come through our windows.
—Jeremiah 9:21 (NKJV)

A society, growing sicker and sicker, yet ever more powerful, has remade the reality of the world to be the backdrop for its own sickness.
—Guy Debord, *The society of the stage*

It is very common for humans to develop things with the best of intentions and for them to have unintended, negative consequences. It is particularly important for us to talk about this now as we may be the last generation that can remember life before.
—Justin Rosenstein, the inventor of the *like* button on Facebook

No one today could dispute the great advantages of the new media in communication, information, and access to culture in all its forms; and soon, no one will be able to do without it. For society has incorporated them into the way its different structures work, be they social, administrative, commercial, educational, or even religious.

It is often said that their invention has given us a revolution like that of electricity and the new means of transport. But there is a profound difference between the new media and those earlier inventions that have so changed the life of modern man. No other invention has monopolized so much of our time, day to day, nor required of us such constant attention and action. Nothing else has so greatly changed our conditions and manner of working, invaded our private lives and families to such an extent, or penetrated so deeply our inner life and our subconscious. No other technique has so greatly changed our relationship to space and time, our way of viewing the world, our relationships with others, the way we see ourselves, the nature and rhythm of our work and leisure, the way we communicate, and the structure and form of our intellectual and psychological life. And no other technique, through its influence on all facets of our being, has had such an impact on our spiritual life.

A vast body of publications praises the advantages and benefits of these new media. The object of this book is not to pile on yet more fruitless praise, but to invite the reader to reflect critically on the use of these new means of communication. For such an unusual approach will reveal how they have become ever more invasive, producing many negative effects of which their users are not fully aware, although they may notice them to some extent in their own lives, in their children, and in those close to them.[1]

Although the modern drift of society, with its dark portents for the future, might make us wish for it to change, our aim, at this critical time, is pragmatic. It is to appreciate better the directions in which the new media are leading us and the real and possible pathologies that they may provoke, to learn to master them, and to limit their use where they have regrettable effects.

The aim of this book is first to diagnose the pathologies that the media can produce and how they may develop in every sphere of society—political, economic, and cultural—and in all facets of personal life—bodily, psychological, intellectual, and spiritual. For they may cause great harm to the lives of men and can go so far as to change man's nature itself for the worse.

If we realize how gravely sick is our civilization, we may gain strength to resist. We can gradually reduce our use of the media and so lead to a decline of the industry that profits from them. And as we reduce our use of the new media, society will change, so that we can discover once more the authentically human and spiritual communion that we have lost.

CHAPTER 1

Invasion

Invasion: the sudden and powerful penetration into a country to pillage it and master it. In medicine: the initial stage of an illness from the first symptoms to its full development. Figurative: the sudden appearance of something which takes up much space or even almost all the space.
—ORTOLANG, Centre National des Ressources Textuelles et Lexicales

Definitions

A medium is a means of passing an object, a word, a sound, or an image from one state or one place to another. It is an intermediary. The term "media" has been used for many years to mean the main transmitters of information: the press, radio, and television. The term "new media" refers to more recent means of communication using the digital techniques developed with the computer. An equivalent term is "digital media." Networked computers, tablets, and smartphones are the backbone of the new media, supported by digital photography, recorders, and portable players of CDs and MP3 files. Because they all use screens, one may use the term "screens" to describe them, which allows the television to be included. It shares many features with the new media that we will discuss later.

The word "media" describes both the methods of transmission and their content, for example, the Internet with its sites, blogs, forums, social networks, online games, and the like.

The singular form of the word, medium, has for many years been strongly associated with parapsychology, so here we will generally use the plural: media.

Digital Colonization

Digital media have progressively invaded every kind of activity and every part of our public and private lives. Roberto Casati has described this as "digital colonialism," which he defines thus:

> Digital colonialism is an ideology based on a simple principle: "If you can, you must." If anything, or any activity, can become digital then it *must* become digital. The digital colonists spare no pains to bring new technologies into every facet of our lives, from reading to games, from teaching to decision making, from communication to planning, from the preservation of artefacts to medical diagnosis. The colonialist assumption is taken as read by the colonists. They like its simplicity: it is general, applying equally to any object or activity whatsoever.[2]

Everyone is pushed firmly by society to use the new media. The main pressure is commercial, to buy the hardware, to buy the software, and to participate in "free" activities that generate profit for business through advertising, and the sale of personal data.[3] But governments are also deeply involved in the propagation of the new media. They encourage their use from the youngest age in schools, and make them essential for certain administrative operations. They think it a moral imperative to reduce the digital divide between different classes of citizens: the "superior" class with full access to the media and their "inferiors" who lack it. No corner of the land must be left without coverage for the Internet, the portable phone, and the television, lest some should be excluded and disadvantaged.

To these economic and political pressures is added a peer pressure: everyone should feel obliged to have access to all the media and all the latest gadgets that use them. The new media and their gadgets are not simply means of integration into the community and signs of belonging, but badges of social value and self-esteem.

The Television

The television is one of the modern media yet does not strictly belong to the category of "New Media," despite the high-definition images, which digitization allows. It has already been widely used for more than 50 years and is to be found in almost every home in the world, even the poorest. In both America and France, 99% of all households possess at least one television. Even in Africa, the poorest continent, 85% of households possess a television. In many households the main television, which presides in the living room, is backed up by several more in the bedrooms of both parents and children.[4]

Only a few are able to resist. They are generally in the higher social classes and, motivated by religious, intellectual, or cultural considerations, seek to protect their children from bad examples and evil influence that may distract them from their school work or from more cultivated and social pursuits. They voluntarily abstain, but are seen as eccentrics.[5] In many families the television is on from morning to night, and, even when no one is watching it, it remains as a background that flavors the whole life of the house.[6]

In general, people spend much time in front of the television, 4 hours per day on average over all the regions of the world. The television occupies a large part of the days of the retired and the unemployed, but it also invades the days of working adults, schoolchildren, and infants. Studies have shown that schoolchildren spend more time in front of the television than in front of their teacher, or in interacting with their parents.

It is a cheap leisure pastime that is easy to access. Many people develop an addiction to it, and it can be hard to tear children away from the screen without provoking disobedience, complaints, and screams.

Children become more deeply dependent than adults. They are occupied less by daily duties in the home, and so are more passive and receptive, captivated by the worlds the television reveals to them. Inexperienced, lacking any points of comparison or solid principles, and bereft of critical ability, they are far more permeable to external influence.[7]

It is not true that the television has been supplanted by more recent media. It coexists with them,[8] either in parallel[9] or as their partner. For instance, while the Internet transmits programs live, it also allows them to be recorded so that they can be viewed later with a computer, a tablet, or a smartphone.

Television's impact on children is especially powerful. As Lilian Lurçat has observed: "The television moulds a child from birth. It implants its message unhindered, for the child has no experience which could counter its effects and the restraint imposed by adults is minimal. The social effects of the media are yet more powerful, for they capture the imagination, seducing and shaping it, by associating what they show with the fulfilment of the basic needs of daily life such as eating and relaxing."[10]

Its power of seduction rests mainly on its use of the emotions, which it stimulates by subtly combining the real and the imaginary into scenes that are truly manipulative.[11] The television aims, through our affections, to draw us to participate and to identify[12] with its message.

Furthermore, many studies over the last decades have shown how the image has an overwhelming effect in modern society. It has its own power to impress, which gives it a huge influence on the way we see reality.

Video Games

Video games also merit our attention. They have always used a screen, and nowadays generally use the Internet with a smartphone. They are not insignificant since worldwide statistics show, for example, that a 13-year-old boy spends on average 2.31 hours per day on video games, or around 35 entire days per year, that is, 9.6% of his entire life. The propagation of video games is powered by their developers who profit immensely (presently around $100 million/year), and who thus gain a significant social role.

At first, video games did not depend on the media. No messages were transmitted from one place, or person, to another. They were simple, but as their software developed, they became more and more elaborate. At first, only one player was involved, as in Gameboy and early versions of PlayStation. They were solitary activities, and they were criticized for their individualism that isolated their users, cutting them off from their fellows.

Once these games became interactive and could use the Internet, they could be played online using connected computers and thus became part of the media.[13] They could then be used for role-playing, each player assuming the identity of a character in the game. These new games were much more demanding of time and energy than those that went before. The players had to be continually present, reactive, and perform well. But the games of old have now made a comeback on smartphones, and once more cut people off from their spouses, their families, and their friends.

The Computer and Its Offspring

In itself, the computer is not part of the media, but it has become their main enabler: connected through the Internet to other computers, it allows different users to send each other messages and files, and it can access files from other Internet sites that it can transform and transmit, thanks to the scale of the Internet.

At first, the computer was essentially a tool of people's trade that it changed radically. Now it is everywhere, in industry, commerce, the civil administration, and schools. It has speedily progressed from the public sphere to the private. Its ability to implement other media was quickly exploited to allow it to be used for leisure activities, which assured the rapid growth of its use. Leaving the office for the home, the computer soon became more compact so that it could be carried around everywhere. First were the portables and the laptops. Then came the simpler and lighter tablets that could be used in any situation, and finally the still smaller smartphone was developed.

The Smartphone

There are currently 7 billion smartphone lines in the world for a population of 7.5 billion, a phenomenon that affects even the poorest countries. In poor families, a "portable" is often a priority, and a contract for every family member can strain the budget and increase the weight of debt. Some people have several smartphones, each for a different sphere of activity, personal and professional, so that in some countries the number of portable phones is greater than the population.

At first, the portable telephone was, like a fixed-line phone, for verbal communication, but could be taken and used independently anywhere. Later, it was embellished with extra features, becoming a camera, a video camera, a recorder, a player of audio and video files, and a mini-computer to connect to the Internet and the social networks. Thus, it became a smartphone and now supports a huge number of applications (over 500,000) that enhance its utility in different ways.

The sales increase all the time, since users, driven by subjective[14] and objective[15] obsolescence, feel compelled to replace their smartphone with one of the newer models, which the makers put regularly on the market.[16] The various factors that oblige people to buy smartphones are cleverly manipulated by the suppliers of phones and the network providers. Among the external factors are the abolition of phone cabins, omnipresent advertising, phones whose price is subsidized in exchange for a contractual commitment to a network supplier, and the requirement to have a portable phone for work, or for seeking work. There are also inner factors: the need to be and do as others (which can be seen even in the school playground); the need to be reassured in a world which seems unknown and menacing; a means of self-promotion (for a fashionable and pricey smartphone is an outer sign of being rich, original, and up-to-date); and a palliative for boredom and loneliness.

The smartphone takes up a good part of its user's time, and its presence is absorbed into life at every moment of the day, from rising to retiring.

The Internet

The computer and smartphone allow everyone access to the Internet (or web, or net) at all times and in any place. Also, the Internet has greatly encouraged the development of the computer and the smartphone. For most people, gaining access to the Internet is the main reason for buying them. Their main use, far ahead of work or games, is to surf the web.

The Internet is a worldwide information network that joins together all the information networks accessible to the public. The word comes from "Internetting"—the act of relating different networks to each other. The result may be depicted as a giant spider's web, which gives the name "web" to the Internet. Through the Internet, each local network can instantly access all the others. The most popular Internet sites are the search engines. There are many, but Google of the United States quickly became the most widely used. Feeding a single word into these search engines will find every site in the world, which refers to it and the information given about it. Thus, the internaut is immediately presented with a huge mass of information about his search in the form of text, images, videos, and sounds. Specialized sites have been developed, which cater for all manner of needs and tastes. Online commerce (e-commerce) has invaded the web. Almost all institutions and associations have their site, and many users have their own personal blogs to which they regularly send information.

Email is part of the Internet, allowing internauts the world over to communicate almost instantaneously, and to exchange rapidly and freely their messages and attachments (text, images, sounds, etc.). Almost 215 billion emails are currently exchanged every day. For many people, browsing the web takes many hours every day. (At present, 70% of internauts use the web daily, spending on average 4.8 hours on a computer and 2.1 hours on a smartphone.)

Social Networks: Facebook, Twitter, and the Rest

The social networks, accessed through the Internet, have developed a huge presence over the last 10 years. They have their roots in the discussion forums found on blogs where users of the Internet may exchange their ideas, impressions, and sentiments. They are still widely used, but thanks to Facebook, there has been a real revolution in this world of communication. It allows anyone to have a personal space where anything can be expressed, and illustrated with texts, images, videos, and sounds as desired; and the content can be shared with tens, hundreds, or even thousands of others.

Facebook has now moved beyond the simple exchange of information between "friends" (the term for those linked together) to become, as well, a platform for sharing knowledge between members of project teams or interest groups, be they students, researchers, or businesses.

It was created in 2004 for the private use of students at Harvard, but has now grown to be the second-most consulted Internet site after Google. It has become a veritable social phenomenon, translated into eighty-five languages and affecting a majority of the young the world over. Today, it has over 2 billion users; more than half of them (1.37 billion) connect to the site at least once a day, spending an average of 50 minutes each to post over a billion items online.

Facebook owes its success to everyone's natural need to be in contact with others. This need is often felt acutely in modern society, which for various reasons has weakened social links and deconstructed the family. Thus, more and more people find themselves alone. Social networks are praised for "making the link" that brings people together and creates social contact for the lonely and shy. Those connected with others are encouraged to empathize with their contacts who present themselves as "friends."

Another reason for Facebook's success is that it satisfies the need of humans to feel that their existence and value are recognized by their fellows. So, the personal Facebook page is often used to expose not only one's existence, tastes, and interests, but also, freely, even rashly and shamelessly, all kinds of details of one's private life, even the most intimate, and one's real and imaginary exploits.

Facebook is the model for other networks of this kind. One of the best known is Snapchat, which allows sharing of photos and videos, but which limits viewing time to between 1 and 10 seconds, and leaves less traces than other such media. It is mainly used by those aged between 15 and 25. It currently has 178 million users online daily. Another popular network, Instagram, was based on the same ideas as Snapchat and serves the same user base, but attracts older users. With 500 million users online daily, it is much bigger than its competitor.

Twitter provides a microblog service. Users can post freely short messages called "tweets" on the Internet using instant messaging or text messages. In the beginning, Twitter aimed to allow people to tell what they were doing as they did it. But soon it was used as a place to publish news, links, and brief comments, especially on recent events. Once connected to Twitter, one has access to all the tweets (mini-messages) posted by one's "followers" (those account holders who have so chosen). The better known one is, the more followers one has. Some have tens of millions.[17]

Twitter allows account holders, followers, and subjects to be filtered and sorted, and allows different filters to be used for reception and transmission. Today, 310 million people use Twitter every month, and 140 million every day. Simply in the United States, more than 2 billion hours are spent in total every month on the social media: 2 hours per user per day.

YouTube is often classed as a social network. It is one of the most widely used Internet sites, available in seventy-six languages and eighty-three countries, covering 95% of the Internet users in the world. Every minute, more than 300 hours of video clips are posted online. More than a billion individual users consult YouTube every month. More than a billion video clips are viewed every day. YouTube is a subsidiary of Google, which receives the advertising revenue and exploits the users' data.

Text Messages (SMS and MMS)

From the start, one of the main uses of the mobile phone has been to send and receive text messages of up to 160 characters via the SMS (short message service). Later, this service was expanded to MMS (multimedia message service), which allows files to be attached to the text message—photos, then videos, and short sound recordings.

SMS is very widely used: on average around 200,000 are sent worldwide every second. They are especially popular with the young: an American adolescent typically exchanges around 2,500 per month. This popularity is due to several factors: the sending and receiving are almost instantaneous even when the transmitter and receiver are far apart; the cost is very low, even for messages sent and received abroad. Moreover, these messages are so short that they can be written quickly and easily using poor and sloppy language that pays scant regard to politeness or grammar, and which employs all manner of non-standard abbreviations, most often phonetic.

The text message allows the rapid exchange of brief news, and also helps to make new contacts. In many cases, this is the important part. The content of the message is a pretext. Text messages, and to a lesser extent, emails, are the main drivers of addiction to mobile phones whose use as telephones has become secondary. Everywhere one may see the owners of mobile phones frequently and compulsively stare at their instruments to see whether they have received a new message, or to use it to send a new message. Recent statistics show that 70% of smartphone users check their messages every 5 minutes.

Connected Devices

Finally, there are connected objects, which create a market with the potential for great present and future development, and which seem to give mankind more power over himself and his environment. Those that use a smartphone or an e-watch to measure and record various physiological parameters related to health and physical activity are already very successful. They cater to the needs of individualistic sports, to the fashion for slimming, and to the cult of the body.

Currently, there is fast growth in those related to home monitoring, and the control of domestic equipment and household appliances at a distance.

There are also helmets (Google Glass, Holo Lens, Oculus Rift, etc.) and other such devices, which allow us to plunge, with all our senses, into a world of "augmented" reality, or into a totally virtual universe. In this way, they allow total escape into a kind of "artificial paradise," which some have described as "the drugs of the future."

There are now 4 billion such connected objects used by private individuals. Every day, a further 5.5 million are added. According to current projections, there will be 20.8 billion connected objects by 2020.

CHAPTER 2

When the Medium Replaces the Message

> The medium is the message.
> —Marshal McLuhan, Understanding Media

It is often said that media are neither good nor evil in themselves and that their moral value depends on the use that is made of them. In other words, there is no such thing as an evil medium, but simply one that has been used to evil ends. This is an ancient argument, since it was used by the Stoics[18] and certain Christian thinkers[19] concerning the use of things. Today it is used for technology in general and for the media in particular. The principle is true to a large extent. In a world where the new media are unavoidable, it would be vain and counterproductive to ban children from using them, but it is essential to teach children how to use them well, to select well their content and form, and to respect certain limits.[20] It is also true that among a large number of users there will be those who use them badly and become addicted and sick through their abuse, while others will learn how to handle them so that they are useful and not harmful.

But the problem is more complex than it appears. The discovery and development of various techniques at the end of the nineteenth century and during the twentieth century have given rise to philosophical debates of the highest order. The gravity of the negative effects of some of them may lead us to question their intrinsic innocence. Thus, in his famous book *The Question Concerning Technology* Heidegger strongly emphasizes the dangers of technology. Unlike Descartes, who considered that it would make us "masters and possessors of nature,"[21] he thought that it would instead disinherit us. In fact he went so far as to affirm that the more mankind tries to master technology the more technology escapes his control because of its own inherent characteristics. Each of us can observe how technology, which is supposed to free mankind and to place the forces of nature at his service, has instead, in certain fields, come to dominate and crush mankind while destroying nature itself. Herbert Marcuse opposes the idea that the value of technology depends on its use, and that its power is completely subservient to the will of man. "It is not simply its use; it is the technique itself which is already a domination (of nature and of mankind[22])." In this it does indeed fulfill "a social and historical plan. It applies what society, and the interests who control it, intend for men and for things."[23] However, all these interests are linked to an economic and political superstructure that dominates people and in large measure imposes itself upon them, and of which they are generally unaware. This is even truer of techniques used in communication systems, in which Edward Hall sees "the hidden dimension."[24]

Marshall McLuhan was a pioneer of the study of media and remains a point of reference. He too disagreed with the commonly held idea that the moral value of media and its effects depend uniquely on what use is made of them, everyone being free to choose what to do with them. He observes that every technique that comes into general use creates, little by little, a completely new human milieu, which ends by imposing itself on everyone. The main message of his famous book *Understanding the Media*[25] is summed up in the formula: "the medium is the message."[26] The message carried by any medium seems to be what is important. But according to McLuhan, this is a mirage. The medium itself has a much bigger impact than the message on people's thoughts and way of life. The message changes all the time, which reduces its impact and leaves it with a merely relative importance. But the medium creates a permanent structure, which leaves a deep imprint in society and its members and little by little changes them.

"It is sometimes a bit of a shock" writes McLuhan, "to be reminded that, in operational and practical fact, the medium is the message. This is merely to say that the personal and social consequences of any medium—that is, of any extension of ourselves—result from the new scale that is introduced into our affairs by each extension of ourselves, or by any new technology."[27]

The statement that "the medium is the message" means that it is the medium that shapes the world, determining the scale of human activity and relationships. The content and use of the media are varied and have no effect on the nature of human relationships. In fact, one of the main characteristics of the media is that their content hides their nature.[28] McLuhan denounces firmly the illusion of those who base their judgements on the content of the media, thinking that their value and their effects are entirely within our power to use as we will:

> Our conventional response to all media, namely that it is how they are used that counts, is the numb stance of the technological idiot. For the "content" of a medium is like the juicy piece of meat carried by the burglar to distract the watch-dog of the mind.[29]

Like Marcuse and Hall, McLuhan stresses the power that the media exert on us through their structure and mode of functioning, a power of which we are unaware. "For any medium has the power of imposing its own assumptions on the unwary."[30] Through our unconscious mind, the media have swept us into their system of organization, and we are their prisoners. "Subliminal and docile acceptance of media impact has made them prisons without walls for their human users."[31]

Because the medium is more important than the message: "Technology does not mainly act on the level of ideas and concepts; little by little, and without meeting the least resistance, it changes the interaction of the senses and our models of perception."[32]

More recently Nicholas Carr in a famous book entitled *The Shallows* has shown from his own personal experience backed up by many scientific studies how the Internet, the most widely used of media, changes the structure of the brain and modifies its various functions in depth.

> "One thing is very clear," he writes: "If, knowing what we do today about the brain's plasticity, you were to set out to invent a medium that would rewire our mental circuits as quickly and thoroughly as possible, you would probably end up designing something that looks and works a lot like the Internet .... With the exception of alphabets and number systems, the Net may well be the single most powerful mind-altering technology that has ever come into general use. At the very least, it's the most powerful that has come along since the book."[33]

This analysis could also be applied to the different media associated with the Internet. As Marshall McLuhan realized, the impact of the media extends far beyond the psychological or intellectual lives of individuals to affect the way of life and the thought of the whole of society.

Werner Heisenberg in his essay *La Nature dans la physique contemporaine* observed that, in general, technical developments not only alter habits of life but also the models of thought and the scale of values of the society in which they function.[34]

But even in antiquity there were wise men who were aware of the negative effects that even primitive technology could have on psychological, emotional, intellectual, and spiritual life. The slow rate of development of these techniques in former times may arise less from the incapacity of traditional societies[35] to invent them, and more from a reluctance to put them into practice inspired by a premonition of the devastating effects they might have on the inner life of mankind. A characteristic example of this is the following saying from the treasury of ancient Chinese wisdom:

Tzeu-Koung, a disciple of Confucius, after going to the principality of Tch'ou returned again to Tsinn. Close to the river Han, he saw a man who was watering his vegetable garden. The old man went down to the bottom of the well and filled a bucket with water. Then he carried it in his arms up to the surface and poured it into the ditch. It was hard work for little result. Tzeu-Koung said to him: "There is a way in which you could fill a hundred ditches in a single day without tiring yourself. Would you not like to learn it?" At these words, the gardener stood up and looked at him saying: "What is this way?" Tzeu-Koung replied: "You take a rod of wood, weighted at one end and light at the other. In this way you can draw water so fast that it might be a spring." At this, the face of the old man became dark with anger, and he said: "I learnt from my master that he who uses a machine does his work mechanically. He who works mechanically ends up with the heart of a machine, and he who bears in his breast the heart of a machine loses his native wit. He who loses his native wit becomes troubled in his soul, and the trouble in his soul prevents the Principal from dwelling peacefully in his heart. I am not unaware of the methods of which you speak, but I would be ashamed to use them." Abashed, Tzeu-Koung hung his head and made no reply.[36]

This text is very rich. It shows how technology can mould its user in its image and make him lose certain natural dispositions, troubling his soul and disturbing his relationship with God.

One may also call to mind the way new media can create new needs while giving the impression that they satisfy old needs. Raffaele Simone chooses to speak of them not in terms of "adaption" but in terms of "exaptation" to underline that, in fact, it is the organ that creates the use and not the reverse. He writes of this subject:

> The omnipresence of the media generates such a dense network that amongst its users it produces a gigantic chain of exaptations. The quantity of needs to which this gives rise is so great that it is difficult to explain in a few words. Has our need to speak on the telephone been repressed for centuries, or is it a novelty born of the availability of cheap mobile phones? Where, in the depths of man's heart, was hidden this spectacular desire to communicate which can be seen the world over since the mobile phone has existed? Was the need to send billions upon billions of text messages every day lurking unfulfilled in the depths of our unconscious, or was it created by the simple availability of a technical resource? Was the need to listen to music everywhere and at all times once violently repressed, or did it come from nowhere, generated by the creation of portable music recorders and players? Was there hidden in the dark corners of our souls a need to be seen on line by others, waiting to be expressed, or did this come from the world-wide explosion of digital photography? I believe that the right answer to all these questions are those I have given in second place. If this is so, then modern technology has given rise to a huge exaptation of the species.[37]

However, for many, these new media have become as idols,[38] and their thoughts and feelings are molded by them. The Bible has a premonition of this in Psalm 113:12–16 (LXX): "The idols of the heathen are silver and gold, even the work of men's hands. They have mouths, and speak not; eyes have they, and see not. They have ears, and hear not; noses have they, and smell not. They have hands, and handle not; feet have they, and walk not, neither speak they through their throat. May they that make them become like unto them, and all such as do put their trust in them."

Behind their messages' variety and impact, the media have their own structure and mechanism. Through their requirements of reactivity and rhythm, and through the habits they generate and their repetition, they influence the way we see the world and perceive space and time. They affect the way we organize our lives and relate to reality and to the people we live with, be they far or near. These influences are far from slight. As we will see in the chapters that follow, they modify and format, little by little and in a new way, vast areas of our lives. Our relationship with our body and our physiology (through our cerebral connections, our senses, our reflexes, and our movements) are changed. Our psychological life, with its powers to will and to desire, its imagination and memory, its emotions and sentiments, is transformed. Our intellectual and spiritual lives, the way we relate to ourselves, to others, and to God, are all changed so much that a new type of human being emerges: *homo connecticus*.

CHAPTER 3

The Tyranny of the New Mediators

He causes all, both small and great, rich and poor, free and slave,
to receive a mark on their right hand or on their foreheads,
and that no one may buy or sell except one who has the mark
or the name of the beast, or the number of his name.
—Revelation 13:16–17

I think that most people don't want Google to answer their questions.
They want Google to tell them what to do next.
—Eric Schmidt, CEO of Google, now Alphabet

The New Media as Political, Economic, and Social Reference Points and Their Mediators

The new media have become the basic reference points of politics, economics, and society and act there as mediators. This mediation acts in two ways. The actors in the economy use them as tools to develop commercial activity. They have not simply developed online commerce but have made it impossible to procure certain services in any other way. The same can be said for certain branches of the administration that require the completion online of certain administrative forms.

Owning a mobile phone has become essential to secure transactions for Internet purchases. The dematerialization of transport tickets means that they may soon be essential in this area too, where they are already widely applied.

Payments currently made with credit cards may soon be made through connected objects, which themselves may be implanted in the human body as happens already in the United States. Mediation will then have reached its extreme, which is described thus in the Book of Revelation:

> He causes all, both small and great, rich and poor, free and slave, to receive a mark on their right hand or on their foreheads, and that no one may buy or sell except one who has the mark or the name of the beast, or the number of his name. (Revelation 13:16–17)

Already, certain jobs require the candidate to possess both an Internet connection and a mobile phone, so that the employer may call upon the services of the employees at any time, even outside legal working hours.

The school and university systems also require their students to possess a computer and an Internet connection, not simply as a research tool but as a means of accessing documents. These may be course material from the professors, schedules of work to accomplish, or online tests and exams. Some institutions even demand that their students sign on to social networks to show their motivation and commitment.[39]

Mediation, in all the above cases, takes the form of an imposition by economic and social interests of the possession and use of the new media on their users. This becomes a condition for belonging to institutions and for the institutions themselves to function. On another level, the new media are used in politics, by governments, by states, and by those who seek power as tools of propaganda, of brainwashing, and of surveillance.

From the users' point of view, we see that they do not simply use the new media as mediators because they are obliged to, but also because they feel the need for them as guides where all others have disappeared. Mobile phones have become the means to locate one's geographical position and to navigate using GPS and map software. Every month, a billion people use Google Maps to find their position and their route to their destination. Even within families, mobile phones have become the way to keep in touch, not only with phone calls, but also through geo-localization. In this new surveillance system, children and adolescents find their independence reduced. So, they lack the autonomy required to mature and the feeling of freedom which they need to blossom.

Confiscation of Personal Life

Computers, tablets, and smartphones have come to be seen as devices to guide us in the psychological, intellectual, cultural, and even spiritual realms. They can answer all our immediate questions, which leads to a weakening of our relationships with others. We no longer write or seek to acquire skills, which leads to a certain laziness when it comes to developing our own resources. All this is controlled by large corporations that manage the production, the use, and the content of the new media with the aim of removing our control over our own environment. For instance, connected objects and domestic robots are cleverly presented as easing the material burdens of life, and, playing on the emotions, as a wonderful way of allowing the handicapped to rediscover and retain their autonomy. However, the true aim of these big corporations is to take control of everyday life so as to rake in the profits from the sale of devices and consumables, to fine-tune their economic exploitation, and to gather enormous amounts of data that can be sold on to other corporations. Suppliers of electricity have these aims in mind when they require electronic meters[40] to be fitted. For these meters do not simply measure consumption, but also recognize the different devices connected to the circuit, and the hours when they are switched on. Another example is Google's self-driving car. The driver is to become a passenger, but all this effort is not aimed at ensuring his calm and comfort. Even selling cars is secondary to the main aim, which is to gather as much marketable data as possible on his driving habits, his preferred destinations, his usual journeys, his passengers, the programs he listens to, the music he prefers, etc.

Large corporations also plan to reduce our control over our own bodies. Connected objects linked to the body, the e-watch and its equivalents for instance, are not simply means of acquiring marketable data on the health and nourishment of the body. They also act as coaches for physical activity and as advisers on diet. Millions of users submit blindly to these devices. From their weight, their body fat, their muscle weight, their diet is imposed. Their device imposes their intake of calories, their physical activity, and the number of calories burned, and counts the number of steps they take each day.

The new media guide *homo connecticus* in his choice of what to buy. He is guided by a multitude of sites that compare products and promote the interests of the companies that sponsor them. His choices are confirmed by many subtle suggestions, which are based on the personal data that have been recorded about him and that have been analyzed to reveal his own preferences.

Homo connecticus is thus led to entrust an ever-growing portion of his daily life to the big data collected by the large corporations that run the new media. Not only are his material needs controlled, but also his cultural choices. Even his most intimate life may be entrusted to them through the "dating sites" that promise love to a lonely heart through the calculation of an ideal partner based on his data, and that have grown considerably on the web.

Remote-Controlled Man

The new media are assuming the role of the GPS in the realm of human thought and action. They allow us to find an outer meaning and direction, which once we found within ourselves or in our friends. Philippe Breton has written on this subject:

> A sign of how the media are trying to absorb the world is the way they attempt to become external guidance systems for human action. [...] The media have become irreplaceable for they are now the only place where we can find the information which allows us to decode the different worlds in which we evolve.[41]

In his analysis of modern society, which pre-dates the digital media, David Riesman perceived the change then taking place between the *inner-directed* man and the *other-directed* man. The former carried within himself a stable system of values that was like a gyroscope to guide him through life. His values were inherited from his family, and were part of a tradition, so that he was also *tradition-directed*. Modern man, however, was *other-directed*, and depended on external systems for orientation and guidance through life. He had lost his gyroscope and needed radar.[42]

It follows from the above that the new media have created a system of estrangement never seen before, while projecting the illusion that they increase our power and freedom.

CHAPTER 4

⌒

Shrinking Distance and Time

Everything ! Right now !
—A slogan of the student revolt of May 1968

For my days have disappeared like smoke …
—Psalm 101:4 LXX

Shrinking Distances in Space and Time

All the new media have this in common: they alter profoundly our relationships with space and time. These form the framework of our present human existence. Through space, we perceive all things that are outside ourselves, and through time, both things outside ourselves and those within. The way we see things, other people, and ourselves depends greatly on this relationship. So do our will, our feelings, and emotions that may be present or absent, stronger or weaker according to the distance and time that separate us from their objects.

Overall, the new media shrink the space and time that separate us from people and things. We can place them, hear them, and see them immediately wherever they may be in the world. In a certain fashion, partly virtual, partly real, we can meet them without having to travel any distance with the various constraints that involves, and without having to wait.

A False Impression of Freedom and Omnipotence

When man feels that he is released, even partly, from the constraints of space and time that belong to his condition, he feels free and powerful. He may even feel all-powerful and, like God, to be present in different places at the same time. A videoconference can bring together at the same time, in the same room, and on the same screen people from New York, Paris, Moscow, Beijing, and Sydney. And each of these people may, at the same time, with television or Internet, follow events taking place elsewhere in the world with a time lag if need be.

The new media also facilitate the seemingly divine ability to act on objects at a distance, at any time: by sliding one's fingers over the smartphone one may close the shutters of one's house in Burgundy while holidaying on a beach in the Maldives. E-commerce allows us to acquire with the least delay any object made anywhere in the world. And we can have instant access to libraries the world over and rapidly obtain books and articles in digital format that could only have been acquired as paper copies and with difficulty in former times. In many ways, the Internet seems to place the world at our feet.

However, as we shall see, the elimination of distances does not abolish space itself, and virtual contacts or encounters create new distances. Just because we do not need to move, space does not disappear. Instead, our encounters lose much of their content and thus increase our solitude. By not having to wait, we gain time; but we lose the psychological and spiritual benefits of waiting: patience, the increase of desire and joy, and the feelings that come from delayed satisfaction. We feel more joy when we arrive at a mountain top on foot than when we are just left there by a helicopter.

In any case it is by no means sure that the media make us gain time. Shortening time makes it pass more quickly, so we have less of it, as each activity is lived less intensely. Moreover, the new media multiply the tasks we may perform leaving us too little time for all of them. The power gained over things is usually restricted to objects and is paid for by the power the media acquire over us when they don't simply deliver us into the hands of commerce. The freedom we seem to gain is confined within new limits and therefore appears largely illusory.

Delegation of Time Management to the New Media

It is clear that daily time management is in part delegated to the new media. This is true in professional and private life. New messages arrive constantly, disturbing the even flow of time and changing its organization by requiring the reorientation of activities. This is also true in family life on two levels. Some activities that mark key moments in daily life or that govern its organization begin and end to fit in with the television. As Liliane Lurçat has observed, in modern societies: "The television in the domestic living space tends to become the mistress of the home, the center around which daily life is organized and lived."[43] So in many homes, for the whole family, the times of the meals, bedtime, and sometimes the time to get up are all determined by the television. For the schoolchildren, the same goes for the time for homework. Television news has a hallowed place in many families and regulates the times of meals. Every episode of weekly soap operas must be watched, so as not to miss anything of the story. So they regulate the evening activities, and bedtime is when the last program to be watched ends. As Michel Desmurguet has noted, television time is a substitute for physiological time.[44]

Moreover, the media often distract attention over and above the way they regulate time. A family meal at a given time, or any other common activity, may be disrupted so that one of the family may finish watching his program, while another is unwilling to miss the start of his program. Another will not interrupt watching a movie, and yet another will not stop listening to a CD. Then there are those who must complete an Internet purchase, or reply without delay to their messages. These interruptions to the organization of family life get on the nerves of those who try to organize it; but worse than this, it leads to the breakup of living together.

Time with No Continuity

The new media have changed the nature of time, removing its continuity to make it broken, piecemeal, and scattered. In days gone by, the continuity of time could be felt through the continuity of activities that required unbroken attention for some considerable duration. They had stability and coherence, giving a sense of the continuity of time. This continuity favored these activities. It encouraged concentration so that time could be used effectively and to the full. The results were good, and even if such a full use of time could be tiring, it avoided stress. When it was empty, there could be boredom, but there could also be meditation.

Connected man is sorely tried by today's time, broken to pieces and shards. When he tries to concentrate on one activity, he cannot keep it up for long, but is constantly interrupted. He may then take on multiple activities at once, which results in a stream of incoherent and unrelated events.

The television is a temptation to zapping between channels. But even when one abstains, the zapping is imposed by the producer, who zaps between different camera angles so as not to bore the spectator who is used to discontinuity and constant change in all the other media.

In the office, work is continuously interrupted by phone calls on the fixed line and on the mobile, by emails, which signal their arrival, and by the loud alerts, which signal text messages, tweets, and Facebook postings. Yet more interruptions come from podcasts and RSS, with sound and flashing signals. Then there is the temptation as one sits at the screen to flip away from the work in hand to some other site, to check something inspired by the work, or by something else that comes to mind.

Connected man has a pressing need for novelty and for contact that has been created for him by giving him the means to satisfy it. If he cuts himself off to protect himself, or switches off his alerts, he fears that he may miss something important. Of course these fears are imaginary, but they are encouraged by pressure at work, by the wretched state of human relations in our society, and also by the desire to exist through the media.

This double desire pushes everyone who works with a screen to consult their Facebook accounts and to click frequently on the email box.[45] Of course there is no need, for reception of messages is automatic, and Facebook alerts one to every new "event." Someone reading a text on the Internet is always stopping to look at the links that pop up, and is also distracted by all the sounds and signals to which we have referred. As Cory Doctorow notes, when we switch on our computer, we enter an "ecosystem of technical interruption."[46] And as Nicholas Carr remarks, the Internet is above all an "interruption system."[47]

Bergson made a very pertinent distinction between time (outer and social) and duration (inner and personal). The way we live the one is influenced and molded by the other so that it acquires the same characteristics.[48] *Homo*

connecticus, even when away from all his devices is (de)formed by his habitual interaction with the media. He lives his inner time as a broken jumbled
mess, which makes him lose any natural unity or coherence of his inner life.

Wasting Time

Everyone who uses the new media soon realizes that they consume huge
amounts of time. Often, they are used "to pass the time," to escape from
the boredom that comes from time unfilled. This is true above all for the
television. Although some think that the new media have replaced it, they
have not, but instead have duplicated it or used it as part of their wares.
Many people spend much time every day watching their television. As a
fraction of the hours of the day it is considerable, and even more so when
added up over a long period. Michel Desmurget deduces from published
statistics that someone over 15 spends on average 3 hours 40 minutes every
day watching television. This is 20% of his waking hours and 75% of his
free time. Altogether it amounts to 1,338 hours per year, or around two
months. So, someone aged 81 would have spent 11 years of his life watching
television, or 16 years of his waking hours.[49] To this must be added the time
spent on the Internet, writing emails, text messages, or tweets, posting items
on Facebook, speaking on the telephone, and playing computer games.

Using the Internet wastes time quickly without us realizing it. This
"magical" quality is linked to the multiple physical and mental operations it
requires: flicking constantly from one page to another. As Aristotle showed,
time is intimately linked to movement, which allows the perception of time.
The slower the movement we follow, the more slowly time seems to pass.
Rapid and frequent movements make time pass quickly.[50]

Navigating the web steals time from our lives in yet other ways. Often,
we use a search engine to find a simple piece of information, which should
be quickly available; but the search engine leads us down many false alleys
and into much useless activity before providing what we seek.

The Cult of Speed

Many studies over many years have shown that, in the modern world, the
acceleration of time has led to a veritable cult of speed in every facet of
social life and individual existence.[51] We do everything ever more quickly,

and we expect that everything should be done faster and faster. Modern man is a man in a hurry, consciously and unconsciously. When he fails to hurry of his own accord, he is pushed to hurry. Since the second half of the twenty-first century, the habit of speed has been encouraged by the creation of ever more rapid means of transport and communication; and this has been further encouraged at work by mechanization, which increases the rhythm of production.

For modern society, productivity is a goal in itself. It introduces the ideas of "time gained" and "time lost" with reference to the adage "Time is money." Instruments for measuring time ever more precisely have been developed[52] to extract the maximum profit. Such ideas were completely unknown in traditional societies for whom time did not count and was not counted either. They had no notion of rapidity, which for them had no importance. They moved spontaneously and slowly, or so it seems to us. In those societies, people "had time" whereas in the modern world we are slaves of time. For all our individual and social activities are required to conform to a precisely defined schedule so that they may be better controlled and more profitable.

The new media have played their part in this world wide promotion of speed as a goal. They allow instant transmission of text, images, or sounds; in commerce, the ultra-rapid placing of orders; and on the markets, high-frequency trading. This all encourages the habit of speed, which becomes second nature in psychological life. It creates dependency, impatience, and boredom and disquiet and anxiety when things are slower and do not happen immediately.

Everything! Right Now!

The new media are the means of getting everything right now. They turn us into spoilt children with desires and fancies that, if they cannot be satisfied at once, make us burst with intolerance and frustration. The mobile phone with its text messages and emails allows us to demand something then get a reply at once. The hundreds of channels available on television allow everyone to choose a program that fits in with the interests, the desires, or even the instincts of the moment. The Internet is the same, with its vast quantities of text, images, videos, and music files. Facebook allows instant contact with one's "friends," and Twitter allows the instant publication of an opinion to a great number of users. Finally, the chat rooms allow instant conversation with someone as soon as the need is felt.

The Internet allows us to browse through the wares of most stores and to order whatever we wish to be delivered as soon as possible. The e-commerce sites emphasize the speed of delivery as a selling point since they know that the consumer is impatient to receive his order. Often, they offer not only an express service, but also a premium[53] service, as Amazon does with its Prime option.

This may seem like a space of marvelous freedom, but it also makes a person the prisoner of his desires. Alain Finkielkraut sees such a connected person as: "Shut up in his claims, given over to the instant satisfaction of his every desire and intolerance, a prisoner of *right now*."[54] This philosopher is also concerned that a new kind of human is being formed, incapable of facing hard, objective reality: "The Internet encourages the individual to develop and blossom in the realm of right now, and to see reality as something to be molded. It will be hard to give such spoilt children any idea of limits or measure in life."[55]

Connected man, who has become used to getting anything he wants at once, finds the real world unbearable if it does not satisfy his wishes straight away. This often happens, for his virtual sphere of action is far removed from the real world, which always puts spokes in his wheel.

A World Without Expectation or Desire That Cannot Bear to Be Thwarted

The psychological and existential problems of spoilt children are well known and are caused by their parents satisfying, or worse, anticipating their every whim. In human life, there is no pleasure without pain, no joy without sadness, no happiness without suffering, no enjoyment without frustration, and no satisfaction without expectation. These things are well known to psychologists, and to writers and mystics. The intensity of joy depends on the intensity of desire, which in turn depends on its distance in space or time from its object.

A world where, in reality or virtually, the magic of the Internet provides everything at once becomes a world bereft of true desire, a world without pleasure or joy, without happiness or enjoyment. Moreover, it is well known that a child needs frustration to grow up adapted to social life. Of course the vulgarization of Freud made popular in the 1960s attempts to deny this and considers the instant satisfaction of every desire to be a source of psychological health and well-being; but the system of liberal education based on these principles has been catastrophic: large numbers of children have grown up unable to cope with the inevitable frustrations of social life, forever maladjusted and discontented.

The Problems of Speed

Homo connecticus feels that the speed with which his desires can be expressed and satisfied frees him from the limits of space and time; but his life is limited in other ways that are often more restrictive. The speed of connection and time of response allow instant contact between individuals. The inconveniences of traveling and waiting are avoided, but, at the same time the richness of the encounter is diluted because the reward depends on the effort it requires.

Any request that reaches its destination quickly requires an equally rapid reply. This insistence on an instant reaction, implicit in modern communications, clearly stresses the person at the receiving end; but it also stresses the sender, for he no longer has the leisure to reflect, which flowed from the latency of old-fashioned communication. The stress rises with the number of requests coming in from the new means of communication, sometimes all at once.

Letters sent by the postal service could be considered at leisure, and answered calmly at a favorable moment. The time needed to write, and the time and expense needed to post the letter limited messages to the essential, not so with emails, text messages, and tweets. Their minimalist style allows their proliferation, swamping those who receive them. Replying to all of them correctly is so hard as to be often impossible, and true communication is paralyzed.

The Internet holds out the promise of instant information on any subject. In practice, though, a huge quantity of information is presented to the user, unsorted by his own criteria. Instead, it is sorted according to the commercial criteria of the provider or his clients. Pertinent results are hard to find, so the time spent in searching is far longer than planned as one wanders among the different links the search engine suggests. An amazing amount of time is spent in the search, which is often fruitless. The speed of the false steps in no way shortens the road!

Many other problems arise for the speed of the new media. We have seen how emails and text messages have degraded the form of messages, leaving them without proper style or politeness. This degradation is clearly linked to the desire for brevity in quest of rapidity. Many misunderstandings arise from this rapidity, and many mistakes arise from striking the wrong key on the keyboard or screen. Typing errors are not always corrected since re-reading is seen as a waste of time, hindering quick transmission. Hitting hastily the wrong key can send the message before it is finished, or to the wrong person, or even to a complete list of contact addresses.

Once a letter was written, there was always a delay before it was posted, until the evening or the next morning. This allowed the writer time to re-read it, to reflect and repent, and to correct and improve it where necessary. The ease and speed with which emails can be sent encourages sending the first draft without any pause for reflection.

It is well known that any work well done needs time, and that the finishing touches are most important for the quality of the result. Having speed as their aim, the new media leave little time for the finishing touches, so the search for speed leads to shoddy work. We try to hit our target without having the means to do so.

A World Without Duration

Far from freeing up time, the new media simply shrink time and speed up everything. The result is a world without duration, because everything is always changing and there is no more space between temporal markers.

As Aristotle and St Augustine[56] showed, time has no objective reality but is "a measure of movement." It is defined by the mind's evaluation of a psychological "space" in terms of "before" and "after." In the new media, the "before" and "after" follow each other so closely and with such speed that the space between them becomes so small that our mind can no longer evaluate it. Time is no longer experienced as duration, but as a succession of events too short to have duration.

The Acceleration of Tasks

The use of computers and the new media has not just speeded up time but also the tasks to be accomplished. In every hour, there are more and more jobs to be done, and more and more quickly. In the 1960s it was said that these machines would enable a civilization of leisure.[57] But we now see that this was an illusion, except, perhaps, for the unemployed, who never desired such leisure, which they now enjoy against their will. The idea that IT and modern communication technology would free up our time has also been shown up as a mirage. Everything is faster, but the amount of information to be handled has grown just as much, so, in the end, there is no benefit; but since modern communications allow employees to be contacted 24 hours per day, their leisure time gets eaten up by work, since they can be called to account and given new tasks at any time.

Multitasking

A new method of working is made possible by the new media: multitasking. They allow several things to be done in parallel. For example, it is possible to telephone someone while typing on a computer keyboard, navigating the Internet, looking at emails, correcting images or sounds, or any combination of the above. The PC, with its large range of applications, is well suited to multitasking, and encourages it. In some ways, it is designed for this purpose by allowing various applications to access the screen all at once. It is true that the human brain is to some extent adapted to multitasking. For instance, we can read a book while walking, and as we read it, we can hold it and turn the pages; but these tasks are related, whereas the multitasking encouraged by the new media is totally unconnected.

When two unconnected activities are performed at the same time, they are not done so well. The one who performs them can concentrate fully on neither, and their simultaneous performance increases stress and tiredness. When multitasking involves communication with another person it creates human problems. The relationship of the communicators is troubled by their physical separation. If they were together in the same place, they would not fiddle with their computers, look at the Internet or their text messages during their conversation, for that would be rude and offensive to the other. Alone in the home or the office, one feels hidden from the other, and free to multitask. Yet the multitasker is easily detected by the person at the other end of the line. Frequent requests to repeat words and phrases or questions and the brevity of the disconnected phrases used clearly indicate a lack of attention to the phone call. This behavior shows a lack of respect toward the other that goes against both Christian and human values, and when it is noticed by the other, it will arouse negative feelings toward the culprit.

Multitasking is not confined to the workplace, but for adults spreads out into leisure activities, where professional risk is reduced but where the scope for spoiling human relationships is just as great. The homework of schoolchildren is also affected. Teenagers do it while listening to music through earphones or with the television on, while receiving and replying to text messages or chats with a tablet or smartphone.

There are those who maintain that multitasking develops new skills, but these are shallow and hinder a more thorough approach to each of the tasks and to deep thought in general. Jordan Grafman, the director of the Neuroscience Unit of the National Institute of Neurological Disorders and Stroke, has said: "The more you multitask, the less deliberative you become; the less able to think and reason out a problem."[58]

The negative effects of multitasking on the intellectual performance of those who practice it have been emphasized by Michel Desmurget:

A large fraction of the brain's resources is absorbed by managing the process of *multitasking* and is not available for performing the tasks themselves. Brain scans have shown that the mechanisms of learning and memorization are changed at the most basic level of the neurons in those who are obliged to flit between simple tasks. Over a long period, multitaskers develop problems of attention.[59] They become easily distracted, and surprisingly, less able to move between different mental tasks. Targeted studies on 14 year olds have shown how their homework is done worse and takes longer when they work with a television on in the background.[60]

Most often, those who multitask do so to gain time, or at least to feel that they gain time. But this is an illusion. The expected gain of time is not simply zero, but negative. Although the tasks appear to be done simultaneously, they are not. In reality "all the brain can do in this situation [where several tasks must be accomplished at the same time] is to pass from one activity to another in sequence,"[61] while "each transition comes with mistakes and loss of time."[62] Robert Casati observes the same thing: "Passing continuously from one task to another wastes time at each step, and these small losses of time add up to reduce the time for each of the many tasks attempted."[63]

Less Dead Time—Less Time for Living

Speed, instant access, and just-in-time are the touchstones of the new media and connected man; and speeding up each task along with multitasking creates a way of life with no dead time. But paradoxically, eliminating dead time removes time for living. Man cannot live to the full when he stifles his consciousness with unceasing activity. No more can he live fully in the giddiness of speed, or by surfing the web where he forgets himself, cut off from reality. As we will discuss later, man absolutely needs silence, solitude, and calm to maintain his equilibrium and to be fulfilled. Dead time is when man can take care of himself, can reflect freely, meditate, contemplate, and pray. This is the time he can devote to those dear to him and nourish a true relationship with them.

The Great Illusion

As a pillar of its religion of progress and cult of technology, our society cultivates its great illusion, which is also related to time. It leads modern man to believe that technological progress will enhance his quality of life far more than the machines, the means of transport, and communications of the last century. Since time has such an important place in human life and contributes so much to its quality, he is tricked into believing that technological progress in every domain will free up time, which he can devote to everything that makes him happy in life.

In fact, the opposite happens. It is clear that the quicker the new media work to free up time, the less of it we have. More than anything else, it is the new media that reduce the time available for man's quality of life at work or elsewhere. As the above analysis has shown, they have given rise to a new way of life and have brought about the evolution of a new type of man: someone always in a rush and submerged with cares who frantically pushes himself to do everything at top speed; someone who can no longer act out or live things deeply and who has lost the mastery of the rhythm and organization of his life. The result is *burn out*, the scorching of his body, mind, and soul. He is burnt up in both body and soul, an experience here and now of hell.

CHAPTER 5

☞

The Destruction of Interpersonal Relationships

I think we have created tools which are ripping apart the social fabric.
—C. Palihapitiya, former vice-president of Facebook

Every friend will say, I too am your friend, but sometimes
a friend is a friend in name only.
—Sirach 37:1

When the remote gets too close, what is close becomes remote.
—Gunther Anders, The Obsolescence of Man

The Globe as an Imaginary Village

Marshal McLuhan's assertion that modern media have created a global village has had great success, and the idea persists strongly right up to the present. It seems so relevant; for as we have seen, the new media have set aside distance by connecting people instantly, and making everyone aware of any incident as soon as it takes place. So, we can say: "It's a small world." Facts, stories, and rumors quickly circulate everywhere; everyone publishes his opinions and observations, supported by images, video and audio files, whether he's sure of them or not; and everyone exposes even the most intimate details of his life so that in the world, just as in a village, everyone knows everything. The new media, through the Internet, the discussion forums, Facebook, Twitter, and the like, allow those separated by great distances to "meet" and to form groups of likeminded folk just as in a village or small town, and to discuss matters as though they were together.

But, as we will stress again and again, these encounters and discussions lack the substance of reality. The new media have created a parallel society, partly real and partly virtual, where faces and bodies, with all the rich and subtle messages they might have conveyed, are generally absent. Such people may be always in contact, but each of them is riveted to a screen, and cut off from real people even when they are close by. So, all of them, even when communicating with others, are bound to feel solitude or loneliness, which they try to remedy by frantically consulting their messages, anxiously awaiting the reply, and speedily composing their response. So the Global Village is not a real village, for the neighbors are not real neighbors, the kinsmen real kinsmen, or the friends real friends.

The Arrival of *Homo connecticus* and *Homo communicans*

It is no exaggeration to say that in a short time the new media have shaped a new kind of man: *homo connecticus* and *homo communicans*. Of course every human is by nature "in relation" and "in communication": nearly 2,400 years ago Aristotle emphasized that the human being is a "social animal." More recently, psychoanalysis and personalist philosophy have shown that the human person can only exist and develop in relation to another, and that language is fundamental to this.

But the human person also needs times of calm and solitude for both psychological and spiritual development. In Orthodox spirituality this is known as *hesychia*. It is also well known to psychologists that a man may multiply his relationships with others, so as to avoid facing up to himself and his own "inner poverty" as Pascal put it. Diversions, as Pascal said, are activities which people seek out to turn away (in Latin *divertere*) from themselves. The continuous connection and communication sought by modern man generally serves this need to forget himself. It then becomes an addiction that, just like other addictions, lets him run away from himself.

The new media provide the canvas for a new scheme of life, involving permanent connection through a string of devices. Their user becomes part of them, not simply their adjunct or their servant, but their slave. A person gets no break from the mass of information they provide. Signals and calls come through all the time, and worse, the person has learnt to seek them, feeling bad when there are none. For many of our contemporaries, connection to the media and communication through them are second nature. They cannot imagine a life without them. To live with no television, smartphone, tablet, or computer would, for many, be like living without eating or breathing. Indeed, many articles are now published that recount how a connected individual managed to abstain for a while from these things as though it were a heroic exploit. People don't just wait for a signal to tell them when an email or text message arrives; they also need to consult franticly their mail box to see "no new messages" or their smartphone to make sure that there are no new texts; and Facebook and Twitter must also be consulted to see the *likes* and *followers* and to be reassured of recognition and existence in the eyes of others.

Philippe Breton observes: "It has become usual to present man as a creature wholly dedicated to communication and in thrall to the image, both his own and those provided by the media."[64] Cyberspace and the Global Village appear as the natural habitats of *homo connecticus* and *homo communicans*. The other inhabitants of this new space seem to be their fellow citizens, their neighbors, and their "friends"; but as we will see, these notions are generally inappropriate and illusory.

In the middle of the twentieth century, some American thinkers, like Daniel Bell, Alvin Toffler, and Zbigniew Brzezinski, predicted that following the agricultural and technical waves of civilization, cybernetics would usher in a third wave, full of promise. One of the main theorists of cybernetics (the ancestor of IT), Norbert Weiner, had a utopian and near religious view of his subject. He thought that the disorganization coming from increasing entropy was a diabolical force that threatened modern societies with death. The only hope of escape for humanity would be in a society with a continuous exchange of information and communication.[65] So, Weiner created the "new paradigm of thought concerning relationships which encloses what is real within relationships and relationships within that which concerns information."[66] Wiener confirmed McLuhan's idea that the medium is the message, and went further, proposing that the purpose of a message is to circulate, and that the purpose of man is to make it circulate.

According to Wiener, man has no identity as an individual subject, but exists wholly within relationships that are essentially social. His being arises from the communication that he creates, and his value is measured by the complexity of that communication. Man is no longer considered as a person, who according to Kant is an end in himself, but as a means to an end. In the context of communication he becomes a medium himself. In this way, Wiener's idea of life denies man's personal freedom and his inner world, which are both fundamental qualities of the person. "To live is to take part in a continual stream of influences coming from the outer world and in the forces which act upon it. In all of this we simply represent an intermediate stage."[67] Man can only live as part of a communication network and insofar as he communicates.

Strange as it may seem, Weiner's vision of these ideals of a new man and a new society is anti-humanist. He set himself up as the apostle of a humanity without inner life and of a communication whose form was more important than its human content. Moreover, he failed to see that this society, which was supposed to prevent the increase of entropy, would do the opposite; for it would create a globalized world where values would become blurred and in which all personal, cultural, and religious identities would dissolve.[68] But in some ways, his vision is prophetic: of a permanently connected man completely devoted to communication, living by it and from it gaining his worth.

Communication Without Content Which Is an End in Itself

As we have seen, for *homo communicans*, communication itself is more important than its content. Communication is vital, of first importance. The message sent and its receiver are secondary. It is communication which fills the need, not what is said, read, heard, or seen. This is particularly true of addictions. Those who are addicted to (dependent on) television sit down in front of the set before they know what they will see, or leave it on all the time with little regard to the program. Those who are addicted to the Internet connect to it before they know what they seek, and express their opinion in forums where they have nothing worth saying. Those who are addicted to the telephone use it mostly to exchange trivialities, or to keep in touch. Unlimited time contracts favor such connections, permanent and without purpose. Apart from these extreme cases the need to communicate can also be seen in the need to check continuously one's emails, one's text messages, or one's Facebook and Twitter accounts. It can be seen in the anxiety caused by a lack of messages, by a failure of the computer or Internet connection, or by a smartphone mislaid.

Philippe Breton is one of those who have most strongly censured this dependence of modern man on "communication without content as an end in itself."[69] Before him, Jean Baudrillard also criticized this "communication for communication's sake" whose essence lay not in the message but in the act of communication. This is "a world with no social contact," "always gaping at the sight of its own tenuous existence."[70]

Hypercommunication as a Fake Escape from Solitude

Connected man's hyper-communication, by emphasizing the form (communication itself) over content (the message), shows quite clearly its main aim: to be a way of escaping loneliness. It is hardly surprising that the new media, which allow communication at will, have developed in a society like ours where social bonds are much weaker than in a traditional society. There is conflict between generations; families are dispersed; marriage is in crisis and unions are unstable; and more and more people, especially in cities but also in the country, live alone, not only in old age but also when still young. People are physically and psychologically isolated. Their loneliness is reinforced by the loss of common standards and values that once allowed deep relationships to develop naturally. The isolation of teenagers is reinforced by misunderstandings between generations. Changes in society, of values and of technology, take place rapidly, and the parents adapt to them much less easily than their offspring.

Paradoxically, hyper-communication does not cure the problem of loneliness, but to some extent makes it worse. As we will see, it encourages superficial relationships which do not touch the deeper levels of the personality where loneliness is felt most strongly. The contact it offers is virtual, not allowing persons to relate at the deepest levels of their being. This lack of fullness in relationships is felt qualitatively and drives the quantitative multiplication of contacts in a wild chase, which never reaches its goal.

The New Means of Communication as Obstacles to Communication

Paradoxically, the new means of communication are often means of avoiding communication or of poor communication, and obstacles to communication itself. It is clear that the brevity of text messages and tweets limits their content and eliminates shades of meaning, subtlety, and any conventional politeness in their introduction or conclusion.

Face-to-face conversations between people rarely last more than a few minutes without being interrupted by the ring of one of their mobile phones. The call is almost never left to ring out leaving the caller to ring later. Instead, it is given priority over the person to whom one is speaking. The flow of the conversation is interrupted, breaking it down into loosely connected fragments.

The same problem arises when, at home or at work, there are two telephones (a fixed-line phone and a mobile phone for instance). The conversation is often interrupted suddenly by the interjection: "Excuse me. I must ring off. There's a call on the other line." Being cut off in this way leaves the impression that one is less important than the more recent caller. And the one who cut you off did so thinking that the new call might be urgent and more important, which is rarely the case.

Restriction of Community Life

The weakening of community life is both a result of the new media and the reason for their success. In some ways the development of the mobile phone is linked to a downgrading of community life. A contemporary essayist observes: "If we need an electronic mediator to communicate, it is so that we may be conformed to a world which splits us up and shatters our lives."[71] The mobile phone makes a link in a society where the bonds between persons are strained through the impoverishment or disappearance of community life in towns, in cities, and even in villages. Family life is losing its cohesion in modern Western societies. Grandparents are excluded from the immediate family circle while marriage is in crisis, with more and more single-parent families and people living alone.

At the same time, and more forcefully, the new media restrict community life even where it might exist. They may even be blamed for the break-up of marriage and family life and in part for the downgrading of other forms of community life.

When radios were introduced, they often replaced family conversation at meal times. Their place as usurpers is now taken by the television whose influence is especially strong in households where the news is watched during the meal. It is often watched with religious attention as studies of the question have shown.[72] Children's programs and adult programs separate the generations for long spells each day, while the programs watched together kill almost all conversation. Everyone is glued to the screen, paying little attention to anyone else, so that interpersonal communication is reduced to a minimum. In many families, where there is a television in each bedroom, the members are also separated physically.

Surfing the Internet has the same effect. In many families, one of the spouses complains of being supplanted by the computer in the heart of the other. The concentration needed to play a video game brings the player to a truly autistic state for long periods, deaf and blind to his surroundings. Less demanding games saved on the computer or accessed online by a smartphone also isolate people. Indeed, it is common to see couples seated beside each other without speaking or even glancing at each other, and playing instead with their smartphones or tablets.

Messaging and phone calls with mobile phones have the same effect. They separate couples, families, and groups of friends as one may easily see. Even in the playground, the children no longer play together but spend their time using their mobile phones. Meetings, meals among friends, and even religious services are affected by this habit. Everyone communicates all the time with many people, but not with their neighbors close by. Philippe Breton has rightly said that we live in "a society where people communicate much but meet little."[73]

We even observe that "what was intended to bring people together leaves the vague feeling that it separates them more than ever."[74] This is not just because everyone, engrossed in the media, is cut off from those close to him. Worse, even when they are physically close, they always give priority to the calls of the media, which separates them psychologically from those close by. Any relationship between them is constantly interrupted, so that they are close physically, but not in reality. They are not in touch, person to person. The new media allow contact at all times and have created social networks which allow their members to be instantly and permanently in contact with tens, hundreds, or thousands of "friends." But the multiplication of contacts and messages, we might say "hyper-connection and hyper-communication" that these allow, results in an impoverishment and degradation of the communication between persons really in touch in their true environment. In many cases, it ends by leaving the individual more isolated than ever before.

In one sense, people do not deliberately cut themselves off from their surroundings and their companions. It just happens that when they receive messages or other temptations to connect; they take no trouble to resist, but simply give in as though the virtual contact proposed must be more promising than the real contact they are actually experiencing. But in another sense, modern man's tendency to cut himself off from the real environment by using the media shows that he has difficulties living with others. This is one reason for the crisis of marriage as a vow of durable union and even of cohabitation as a couple. We find it hard accept the self-sacrifice that any kind of close union requires. And all this takes place in a hedonistic society which gives absolute value to individual desire and pleasure.

Unable to truly live with others, *homo connecticus* creates his own world, a virtual one, in which he shuts himself up. It gives him pleasure for it is made to his measure, free from the constraints of the real world and the need to relate to others. There, he is master. Philippe Breton observes:

> The price of the apparent ease of communication through the media [develops] unfitness for direct encounters. [... .] In the universe of "total internet" each individual is steered towards creating his own vital space where he will be answerable to no one. Everyone becomes the monarch of his own territory and has no further interest in entering the space of another.[75]

The new community brought about by the new media turns out to be less the "global village" predicted by McLuhan, but rather a universe where everyone becomes his own little world.

The Disembodiment of Relationships

Virtual relationships facilitated by the media have to a large extent replaced real relationships. Of course, "virtual" is not a synonym for "unreal," and virtual relationships do have their own existence, but just less real. In a virtual relationship through the media the person is not fully present in all his reality, but only through his voice, what he writes, and, maybe, his image. It is striking that in almost every relationship enabled by digital media, bodies are absent: they are disembodied. Isaac Asimov, pushing everything to the limit, prophetically described such a disembodied world in his novel *The Naked Sun*,[76] where bodies are inactive, invisible, and useless.

In encounters where the body is excluded, even as an image, some may feel more at ease. One may feel less inhibited in a telephone conversation than in a face-to-face meeting, and still less so in a discussion forum. Digital media are often praised for helping the shy, inhibited, or neurotic in their relationships. They are seen as a therapeutic means of socializing or re-socializing these people, but there is not much truth in this.

The fundamental causes of difficulties in inter-personal relationships are not treated by this new way of communication. Instead, it is used to hide what the person cannot handle—bodily presence and what goes with it, fear of the other—by fleeing any meeting with him, especially face-to-face with the risk of revealing who one truly is. So, the causes are not treated but become more deeply rooted. Moreover, the apparent socialization takes place in a world parallel to the real world. It is disembodied, removing what gives an encounter its fullness and makes it authentic and true.

The body contributes to the truth of an encounter for it is easier to deceive with words when the body is absent. The body enriches an encounter. Its attitudes, gestures, and body language can greatly enhance the words, and even go beyond them, confirming them or showing them to be false. The body adds emotional content to the words, through its intonation, and enlivens them with its rhythm. The eyes, especially, express the inner soul of the person. In this way, the very fact that they disembody the word means that the new media strongly contribute to the disembodiment of relationships.

The Impoverishment of Interpersonal Contacts

The new media have not eliminated relationships between people. Instead, they have multiplied their quantity while sapping their quality. Since contact can be made by SMS or email, direct contact is less important or even unnecessary. But clearly these contacts through the new media lack the same richness. They are remote, without the real presence of the other. As we have already shown, the emotional force of real contact is absent, as is the richness of body language, the expression of the face, the tone of the voice, and expression through gestures. In addition, the messages of the exchange are short and simplified as is evident nowadays in almost all emails, text messages, and tweets. Finally, all these ways of communication minimize or eliminate every formula of politeness, introduction, or conclusion, which was used in conventional correspondence. Although they may seem to have been mere formalities, in fact they helped to make and maintain a link that went beyond the main content of the message.

Abbreviated style is especially common in text messages and tweets, but is also the general rule in emails, even though they allow the use of a more developed style and normal linguistic constructions. An email, quickly sent and quickly received, conforms to the overall context of rapid communication even when it is not urgent. The writers of both the first message and the reply, often driven by the compression and acceleration of time, feel the need for brevity, and the message is distorted in several ways:

1. The message is less developed than a normal letter, and subtleties of meaning are lost.
2. Reducing the message to its bare bones, the aim sought, often gives it an authoritarian tone, like an order, with scant attention to the politeness due to the receiver.
3. The polite phrases which normally open and close a letter are abbreviated as much as possible to the merest formalities or omitted all together. It is true that the introduction and conclusion to a normal letter also have a formal character, but they permit a large range of expression of different feelings and of different degrees of respect in accord with the social rank of the correspondents and their closeness or distance.
4. The ephemeral nature of the message makes it resemble words spoken rather than written words which remain. And the writers' preoccupation with the content rather than the form leads to a very poor style compared with the style of a letter. It is poor on the literary level and also on the human level to which it is often closely linked.[77]

A New Individualism

Modern man is isolated from his fellows who are really present beside him so that he may make virtual contacts instead. Insofar as this is deliberate, it is an example of a new kind of individualism which is perfectly aligned with the general trend to individualism in modern liberal societies.[78] Philippe Breton sees here a double paradox: first, the fact that "the global generalization of tastes, standards and behavior which creates a universal public space" goes hand-in-hand with "the individual turning in on himself"; and second, the fact that "modern man [...] favors the frantic search for virtual and unreal encounters whilst refusing, even with disgust, any true encounter with his fellows."[79]

Widespread Autism

The mark of autism is not simply turning in on oneself, but also what underlies this behavior: panic at the idea of any real encounter with another individual. Thus connected man may be seen as doubly autistic.

First of all, the use of the new media leads to separation from others, isolation, and turning in on oneself. The new media appear to shrink distances, but, as we have seen, put everything at arm's length. This makes direct encounters in flesh and blood with others difficult and hinders face-to-face contact.

Second, modern man uses communication less as a means of drawing close to others and more as a way of admiring himself by using others. For many, Facebook is purely a way of measuring the esteem, measured by *likes*, which others bestow, and Twitter by the number of *followers*. These sites are ways of showing off to others and gaining their esteem. The new media are most often mirrors of me.

In the same way, discussion forums are often not really a means of exchanging views, but simply a way of promoting one's ideas or merely one's presence; for most of the posts are reactions to others or just empty words. Michel Béra and Eric Mechoulan write: "A discussion group on the internet does not encourage interest in the other, or teach the art of listening. Instead, its virtual character allows what is impossible in reality: everyone speaks at the same time without paying the slightest attention to anyone else and never being obliged to pause."[80]

Real Relationships and Virtual Relationships

The new media have replaced real relationships big time by virtual relationships. As we have already seen, virtual relationships are not entirely unreal. They at least have a digital reality in the form of text, images, and sound files. But since there is no direct face-to-face contact with the other, the contact is imperfect and incomplete. Filtered by the media, it lacks the concrete reality of persons fully present to each other. The reality may be far removed from its representation.

On top of this, the virtual relationship may be edited, either by the sender or by the media themselves. We have already mentioned how the television manipulates the news, and the ever-increasing number of tele-reality programs. Although these are supposed to be reality filmed in the raw, they are in fact either staged according to a plan, or edited after the event to fit in with it. Those who take part in discussion forums often play a role, behaving as stage characters rather than themselves, and often use pseudonyms. Just as with Facebook, the participants hide their true selves, trying to present to the world an image which is to their advantage and overdone. It hides their defects and exaggerates their real and imaginary qualities.

The False Friends of Facebook

A special case of virtual relations is that of the "friends" of Facebook. "Friends" is put in quotes for two reasons. First, the word is cunningly chosen by the creators of this network to give the impression that it opens the door to true friendship, and real communities and networks of friends. Such a claim is bound to attract subscriptions in a society whose natural communities have dissolved, and where more and more people find themselves isolated and lonely. For them, the social networks seem to be the answer.

Second, the notions of friend and friendship have become completely degraded. A true friendship needs depth and time to mature. Then much care must be taken to maintain and preserve it. As the wise son of Sirach says: "If thou wouldest get a friend, prove him first and be not hasty to credit him" (Sirach 6:7). True friendship is a form of love, founded on knowledge in depth, on affinities of taste and ideas, and the ability to listen and give help. Such things are impossible to achieve or experience through media contacts, almost always superficial and speedy. On Facebook, a simple click is enough to claim friendship with someone. What value have such claims so lightly entered into?

Everyone wants to be loved, and *homo connecticus* tries to find love through a collection of *likes*, *friends*, and *followers*. He believes that their numbers, which he checks continuously, measure his popularity and the value and importance that he thinks he has for others. However, these numbers can easily be inflated artificially. Cinema stars and pop stars use their fan clubs and commercial services to increase their numbers of Facebook *likes* or *followers* on Twitter, and the number of their videos watched on YouTube. And what value do these numbers have when set beside a real friendship or sincere admiration, whose true measure is their quality? There are many who have hundreds or even thousands of "friends" on Facebook but have not a single true friend in their lives.

The developers of Facebook never for a moment wished to create links of friendship between their users. The aim of the *like* is to flatter the ego of the one who receives it. His narcissism is exploited with a purely commercial aim to make him dependent on the network. Sean Parker, the former president of Facebook, recently said that the site "exploits a vulnerability in human psychology." This is done through a feedback loop of validation, which encourages people to publish all the time to gain more *likes* and comments. He added: "The inventors, creators—it's me, it's Mark [Zuckerberg], it's Kevin Systrom on Instagram, it's all of these people—understood this consciously. And we did it anyway."[81]

Discussion Spaces and the Problem of Pseudonyms

From its earliest days, the Internet has hosted a variety of sites dedicated to discussions in real time or after the event. There are discussion forums, chat rooms, or spaces for comment after an article posted on a blog. If each contributor brings something new to the discussion which complements the other contributions, then the experience of the participants and their readers may be enriched. Different viewpoints, new facts, and knowledge are progressively added to the record. The subject can be seen from new angles that provide deeper insights, so that the final result may be quite a complete study of the question. The contributors may help each other. Those who know more and have greater experience and understanding can help the beginners who lack knowledge and experience but seek it. Sometimes false ideas can be set right through such exchanges. Lonely people may feel linked and united by faith or by shared ideas and opinions, so the forum becomes an extra means for contact and unity.

However, alongside these positive factors, and related to them, these discussion spaces almost inevitably have a negative side. They cause problems for those who run them and for those who participate, which are mainly linked to the participants' use of pseudonyms.

1. A problem arises from the degree of competence and authority of the contributors. It is rare that any of the contributors to forums or blogs have any recognized competence in any of the subjects discussed. Those who are truly competent have other ways of expressing their views. They generally

shun forums and blogs since participation takes so much time which they can ill afford. Moreover, those who are expert in a particular field are not willing to see their judgments contradicted by lightweight arguments put forth by the less experienced and less competent, who hide behind their pseudonyms when boldly and recklessly advancing their opinions.

The pseudonym allows anyone to express views about anything even when lacking any competence or authority. And in many discussion spaces there are contributors with nothing to say who express themselves simply for the sake of it. A hierarchy develops spontaneously among the participants, which reflects the confidence and style with which they express themselves and the number of facts they allege. This deceptive ranking bears no relation to their knowledge or competence. But in the end, their arguments lack quality because of their poor mastery of the whole area under discussion. They lack discernment and misunderstand certain things. Often they lack rigor and precision in their presentation of ideas. Overall, the way subjects are treated tends toward the lowest common denominator. It could be said that pseudonyms are not to blame for this, and it would be all the same if the participants were not anonymous. However, pseudonyms make things worse since they prevent contributors being identified as personally incompetent and thus abolish all balance and restraint.

2. A second problem, linked to the first, is that the subjects discussed are relativized. Anything stated in a forum will always be contradicted by a statement which may lack authority or relevance. Even when a good argument is set forth, well-reasoned, and backed up by sound evidence, it is almost bound to be contradicted immediately, deformed, and twisted by someone hiding behind a pseudonym, a cloak for levity and irresponsibility. The course of the discussion usually weakens any authority the contributors may have, relativizing the content and leaving an overall impression of vagueness and uncertainty. In the end, one may often ask what the use of it all was. The moderator of a French blog which has been widely followed for years recently confessed: "Personally, I never participate in forums. There's no point in them."

3. A third problem is that pseudonyms encourage a lack of respect for other contributors and allows them to be judged and insulted with impunity. There is often much verbal violence which the moderators let pass. At best, they wish to keep censorship light and to avoid annoying the contributors by cutting them off. At worst, they simply wish to enliven their blog.

Writing under a pseudonym, a contributor has a sort of double personality that prevents his conscience feeling how bad and unethical is his behavior toward his fellows. Were the contributors to write under their own names, they would never indulge in such behavior. In general, the pseudonym acts as a cloak for any outrage, intemperance, or exaggeration. The contributor escapes from the limits of courteous behavior that are normal in society, and does not fear being unmasked and judged by his fellows.

The discussion space where the contributors all have pseudonyms is like a group of children with no social norms, no self-control, and no measured thought or language. It is like a playground where the children insult and hit each other with total abandon, an outlet for all the passions.

4. Another problem is the cheating and trickery, which pseudonyms facilitate. It often happens that a contributor uses several different pseudonyms, not only in different groups, but also in the same. This allows him to give the impression that his idea is supported by several different people. It also allows him to express an idea in several ways, for instance in well-written prose, then in a more colloquial style, and finally something in between the two. Sometimes this expresses different sides of the contributor's personality. It can also enliven the discussion and change its direction. This technique is often used by the moderators or managers of the group. All this leads to the adoption of ambivalent or even schizophrenic positions. It tricks those who read the discussion and the other contributors into naively believing that each pseudonym represents a separate person.

5. This brings us to the phenomenon of trolling, well known in all discussion spaces. In terms of the Internet, a troll may be positive: someone who joins a discussion or debate with the aim of self-promotion; or a troll may be negative: someone who tries to start and encourage arguments and generally disturb the equilibrium of the discussion group.

The word "troll" has two different etymological roots, each of which is significant. In Scandinavian mythology a troll is an aggressive, malicious, and monstrous creature. It can also mean a lure used in fishing.

Trolls, of course, use one or preferably more pseudonyms. With two or more, a troll can discuss something with himself to enliven things and steer the discussion in a particular direction. A troll is unhappy with the way the discussion is going and seeks to change it from within, or to degrade it to the state where it becomes unsustainable and must be abandoned. Such a person is an outsider who does not agree with the consensus of the group. He may be someone who belongs to another group, or has other ideas. He disguises himself and uses various stratagems to avoid detection: a false naivety and various different pseudonyms that indicate different ethnic origins, ages, and sexes.

Such acts are full of lies and trickery and, in most cases, perversity, which show up in the stimulation of individual conflicts or the creation of general discord, often purely for pleasure. Pride and vanity are often the motives for trolling. The troll tries to measure his strength to direct the discussion and to push the other contributors to act as he desires. He tries to score points off the others, whom he considers as role-play characters and does not respect as persons. He sometimes tries to enhance his profile, trying to be interesting when he has nothing to say.

6. The use of pseudonyms depersonalizes the contributors and makes them unreal. This encourages them to manipulate each other as objects and even to manipulate themselves. Michel Béra and Eric Mechlouan have written on this subject:

It is clear that it is even easier to treat another person as an object when he has no material presence, and above all, no face. The one with whom I talk is perhaps just a shadow and certainly less than a man. The discussion group allows me to show my mask but does not show that I have any interest in the other masks or even less in what they may hide. It is no accident that sex has had such success on-line, for sexual activity, like no other, allows one to use another person as an object to satisfy one's desires. When the face of another person can be seen his humanity still has some effect; but when it disappears, there is nothing to distinguish what remains from the world of things. We still do not suspect how much the use of the internet trains us to forget what is human.[82]

Using a pseudonym might seem to be a sign of modesty; but where is the modesty when an unknown person hides? It may be more a case of pride, hoping to pass for better than one is. There may also be fear of being exposed to the judgments of one's fellows, showing an inability humbly to accept what others see in us. It may also be a sign of cowardice, an unwillingness to say certain things openly and personally to assume the ideas one puts forth and the words one uses. It also signifies an inability to take responsibility for ideas or words especially when they are outrageous aggressive or insulting.

As we have observed several times, the use of a pseudonym is a lie to others, a piece of trickery. To pretend not to be the person one is, but a character (the original sense of *prosopon* in ancient Greek, which now means a person) or a mask, falsifies one's relationship with oneself and with others. Adopting a pseudonym means that one does not relate to others as whom one is, thus falsifying one's own side of the relationship. From their side, others cannot perceive truly the identity of the one to whom they should relate, so their relationship is equally false.

Very often, accepting the use of pseudonyms by oneself and others indicates an underlying desire to avoid relating to another in one's true self so as to manipulate him with a clear conscience. There may also be other, pathological motives as the psychiatrists Michel Hautefeuille and Dan Véléa have emphasized. One is the wish to avoid face-to-face confrontations; another, even more neurotic, is to escape the fear of other people and the real world in general: "Through his borrowed, entirely virtual identity, the subject hides himself from the outer world which he feels or imagines to be dangerous, frustrating or nightmarish."[83]

Another manifestation of psychopathology is the use of pseudonyms to construct a fictitious identity for oneself in discussion spaces. The ideal fictitious identity has none of the real defects of the individual and is adorned with qualities that he has little chance of ever acquiring in reality. This creates a double personality evolving in two parallel existences. The greater the time spent on the media compared with time spent in real life, the more this schizophrenia becomes dangerous.

Irresponsibility in Relationships: Slander, Backbiting, and Bullying

Relations between persons are also affected by the way the new media facilitate slander, backbiting, and bullying on the Internet and through social networks. They make such behavior very easy to implement, and in general promote irresponsibility in social contacts. They encourage the virtual world to seem different from the real world and to have no effect on it, so that what is done in the virtual world never implies any real responsibility. In other words, using the new media is always seen more or less as a game.

Students in school may in their leisure time use the new media to bully the weak. They reveal their secrets; they decry their behavior, real or imagined; they speak evil of them and insult them. The scapegoats and victims still exist, who in former times were insulted to their faces, or beaten up at the school gates. But nowadays the bullying is done through messages on the social networks. Since these attacks are psychological, indelible, hard to contradict, and have such a wide circulation, they do far more harm. The victims are generally adolescents with a fragile psychology. They easily lose self-esteem and suffer if they feel the slightest weakness, real or imaginary, becoming deeply destabilized and depressed, or even suicidal.

This behavior has spread far beyond the playground and affects adults. Each, with his computer or smartphone, becomes an all-powerful master who, from vengefulness, jealousy, or sadism, makes or destroys the reputation of others by posting on multiple Internet sites or the social media, text files, photos, video and audio files, all of which may be "re-touched."

The Internet: The Trash Can of History

Once an article has been posted on the Internet, it has every chance of remaining there for ever. It is often copied onto other sites, multiplied, and archived, and leaves indelible marks. This can be a problem, so e-reputation services have appeared in recent years which promise, for a fee, to remove from the Internet those files that might compromise a person's image and reputation. But try as they may, they often do no more than hide the compromising material, or create new material that contradicts it. More than ever we should heed the dictum: "The written word remains." And, one may add, photos and videos too. It is not without reason that Alain Finkielkraut described the Internet as "the trash can of history," for it is not just the best which remains, but also the worst.

Malevolent people often post slanders and lies on the Internet which can remain there indefinitely to stain and destroy the reputations of their targets. They can also search through the data on the web, which includes every past edition of the newspapers with all the articles they contain. There they can find accounts of past crimes which have been dealt with by the courts, to display for all to see, although the perpetrators may have paid their debt to society through the sentence they served and repented of their wrongdoing, or may even have been innocent and had their case dismissed. The Internet then appears as a world which never forgets or forgives.

CHAPTER 6

☞

Evil Encounters

Mine enemies compass my soul round about.
—Psalm 16:9 LXX

Every kind of navigation has its danger zones. The Internet is, in part, a place of meeting and discovery, but also in part, a place of evil encounters and perdition. Every country and city contains such zones, and always has. What is new is that the new media, the television, and especially the Internet have revealed them to all. They make them easy of access and allow them to enter into the home and to dwell there.

The Internet: A Place of Impunity Where No Law Applies

Except for those rare cases where a state blocks the sites of extremists and other dangerous people, anyone can publish on the Internet whatever they like about any subject whatsoever. There are personal pages, blogs and forums, and also e-commerce sites where both legal and illegal products are sold. It has often been said that the Internet is a place of impunity where the law's writ does not run. Tracing and excluding those who abuse the Internet is made difficult by the huge number of sites and sources of files. Simultaneous transmission, as in peer-to-peer networks, and the applications like Tor and Freenet that allow identity to be hidden make the task harder still. Indeed, through applications such as Tor, the *dark net* is enabled, a parallel, underground invisible world where all kinds of illicit activities flourish—arms and drug dealing, for instance—which can grow, hidden from the eyes of the police.

Promoting Sex and Violence

While it is true that the new media did not create violence nor start the taste for what is commonly called sex, they nonetheless have done much to nourish and develop them, making them seem normal.

The Television

Many studies have demonstrated the negative influence of the television on violence and sexuality.[84] Teenagers are clearly the most affected, but young children are not spared either. Children between 4 and 10 years old spend 80% of their television time watching programs for the general public,[85] and zapping between the multitude of channels allows access to the most varied choice of program.

An American study has shown that a young person watching television 2 hours per day sees around 10,000 violent scenes every year. Another study conducted in France by the Conseil Supérieur de l'Audiovisuel gives similar figures. Those watching television are shown on average two crimes and about ten acts of violence every hour. If they watch for 3.5 hours every day, then they see 2,600 crimes and 10,000 acts of violence every year.

The American Academy of Pediatrics has warned that these scenes of violence have consequences: "Exposure to violence in media [...] represents a significant risk to the health of children and adolescents. Extensive research evidence indicates that media violence can contribute to aggressive behavior, desensitization to violence, nightmares, and fear of being harmed."[86] And Michel Desmurget reaches similar conclusions in the long chapter on violence in his book *TV lobotomie. La vérité scientifique sur les effets de la television*:

> It appears that the bad effect of television on aggressiveness is now firmly established scientifically. Every comprehensive study of this subject over the last 15 years has come to the same conclusion. Overall, the violent content of audiovisual media has three effects:

(1) dulling of sensitivity: the spectator gradually learns to tolerate greater and greater levels of violence without flinching; (2) feeling the world to be threatening: the spectator gradually becomes convinced that the world around him is hostile and dangerous; (3) aggression: the spectator behaves with more violence and aggression both short term and long term. No argument has been found to support the idea of catharsis, which suggests that the spectators will get rid of their violent impulses by seeing them represented on the television. [...] The conclusion is unavoidable: by reducing our exposure to violent scenes we help to make the world less violent. To say otherwise shows either a denial of reality or an intellectual swindle.[87]

Scenes of sex on television are equally common. An American study conducted in 2005 showed that 70% of programs for general viewing contain sexual references in 5.5 scenes every hour on average; 77% of prime time programs show 5.9 sexual scenes per hour, and 70% of the twenty most popular programs for teenagers show 6.7 such scenes.[88] One of the effects of this sexual saturation is to trivialize intimate relations. Michel Desmurget hits the mark when he writes:

> The flood of sex which drenches our screens [...] is almost always tainted with completely unrealistic depictions of sexuality [...]. The sexual act is presented by the television as a general rule, which can be indulged wantonly and without risk, and at least half the time between people who hardly know each other. Women are most often presented as objects of desire or satisfaction of lust. They are depicted as willing and passive creatures [...]. On the contrary, men are presented in dominant, almost predatory roles. Their relationship with sex is frequently seen as defining their masculinity.[89]

Adolescents, who repeatedly watch these scenes, gradually and unconsciously acquire a certain image of sexual relations and of what is normal and what is not. Victor Strasburger finds that examples of the ideas acquired from the television are expressed as follows: "everyone sleeps with someone" [...], "adults don't plan their sex" (that is to say that they copulate impulsively at any opportunity), that "everyone has sexual relations" (including those of their age), that "married people often cheat each other," and that "sex is a recreational sport."[90]

This "teaching" is absorbed automatically by the subconscious through the play of repetitions, which makes what seems usual and ordinary pass for normal and normative. Then teenagers add to it other ideas that are equally worrying both psychologically and ethically. Michel Desmurget describes this as follows:

> Behavioral studies have shown that the more an adolescent watches television the more the following tendencies are acquired: (1) to overestimate the prevalence of sexual activity amongst teenagers; (2) to have unrealistic expectations of sexual "performance"; (3) to have a permissive attitude to sexuality; and (4) to feel strongly the need to perform the act. The mark of each of these tendencies can easily be seen in the behavior of teenagers.[91]

The influence of the television on the young for encouraging violence, sex, or other immoral acts is reinforced by its attribution of these habits to its heroes or leading characters. They are portrayed as full of strength and conquering power, winning riches, etc. Without realizing it, the young identify with these role models and imbibe their influence by imitating them. This tends to restructure their psychology and morality with the risk of lifelong effects.

Video Games

Video games are becoming more and more violent and more and more realistic. They often simulate scenes where the player is armed and directly involved. They help to develop aggressive instincts, to trivialize violence, and to blur the distinction between fiction and reality, which all encourage violence in life. Online games are more dangerous than those played alone. They set the player against virtual characters who are not independent, but manipulated by other real people. Real people are set against each other, which further blurs the distinction between fiction and reality.

The Internet

Since the Internet duplicates the television's films and enables online video games, it clearly reproduces the same effects, just mentioned. It has also encouraged the spread of violent videos published by the propaganda sites of extremist groups. But above all it has facilitated the spread of pornographic videos and images that used only to be found in specialized magazines, which had to be purchased, or in films projected in specialized theatres, or on encoded channels late at night.

The propagation of pornography on the Internet has been so widespread that 12% of all sites worldwide are now pornographic, that is to say 4.2 million sites and 420 million pages. Every day, 350 new pornographic sites come online. Every second, 30,000 people connect to these sites and pages. Every day, there are 68 million online searches for these pornographic sites, that is to say, 25% of all requests to search engines, with the word "sex" in every language being the most common of all search terms. Many pornographic sites are free, but are designed as baits to lure the users to sites which charge, or to paying options. Internet pornography is an industry which brought in 97 billion dollars in 2005.

The viewing of sex on the Internet has been studied mainly in America. The results are very significant. Of the 57 million Americans who have access to the Internet, 25 million visit pornographic sites for spells of between 1 and 10 hours per week. Out of these, 200,000 are addicted to pornographic sites and other online sexual material, such a sexual "chats."[92] Viewing online pornography at work is admitted by 20% of men and 13% of women, and 10% of all adults admit to an addiction to cyber-sex.[93] Pornography is encountered accidentally by 79% of young people surfing the web at home.[94] Pornography is a problem in the homes of 47% of all families.[95]

Obviously, young people's encounters with Internet pornography are not always accidental. According to the statistics, 65% of Internet searches conducted by young Americans between 10 and 16 years old are for pornographic sites. An average American school student has looked at 1,400 explicit sexual references per year before leaving school.

Regular visits to sexual sites do not provide an outlet that could improve psychological health and reduce sexual aggression, far from it. Instead, they create addiction and blur the boundaries between fiction and reality, encouraging indulgence in the act and increasing the amount of sexual abuse.

Far from educating the young, as some suggest, such visits to sexual sites degrade the idea of sexual relations by showing them in their most perverted forms, rather than their normal expression, which is foreign to pornography. Youth is taught to see the person as a body, and the body as an object, by depicting sexual relations as a purely physical activity for selfish individual pleasure, completely divorced from respect and love.

The Internet has quickly become one of the enablers of pedophilia by allowing perverts to exchange photos and videos. In 2014 there were 20,000 sites containing pornographic images of children. In 2009 the UN estimated that at any one time 750,000 people worldwide were looking at pedo-pornographic sites. With the social media it has become the favorite hunting ground for pedophiles. The predators most often first relate to children through forums, where they pass themselves off as children. Inhope, a network of fifty-one states concerned about cyber pedophilia, found that the children most affected were those in pre-puberty, 8 to 10 years old for girls and 11 to 13 years old for boys.

Psychiatrists consider sexual addiction as having the same pathology as other addictions—drugs and gambling for instance. But unlike many other addictions it is not simply harmful to the addict, but to others, especially when it involves sexual intercourse,[96] as is often the case.

Ill-Famed Places

From its earliest days, the Internet has hosted different kinds of ill-famed sites, as if the global village was structured like a town with its rough areas full of risk and danger. The difference is that in a real town people must make a conscious effort, and sometimes take risks, to get to these ill-famed areas. But the computer and tablet open immediate, easy, and comfortable access to these areas for the "surfer," offering him a huge array of choice.

As we have seen, evil encounters on the Internet are virtual meetings with individuals or situations that have an evil influence on the way violence and sexuality are seen. They encourage the acting out of what they suggest and may lead to real meetings with sexual perverts—voyeurs, exhibitionists, sado-masochists, pedophiles, and the like. It is also possible to meet swindlers, drug dealers, political and religious extremists, and those who perversely encourage dangerous games or suicidal practices.

Cybercrime

The Internet has become a great arena for what is now called cybercrime. Different factors explain this phenomenon:

1. It is possible for a delinquent to reach anyone anywhere in the world from his computer simply by knowing the target's email address.

2. The target can be easily deceived. There is no physical contact, so with a simple combination of texts and virtual images a false identity can be assumed. Commonly, a false profession with a false address and a fictitious business will be used to sell false objects, false discounts, and to send false requests for credit card details, phishing serving as a bait for thousands of Internet users at once.

3. Impunity is virtually guaranteed. The identity of the transmitter (IIME: international identity of mobile equipment) is easily hidden with the right software encryption combined with false identities and false addresses, making detection very unlikely. Moreover the lack of international agreements that would allow the successful prosecution of cybercriminals allows many of them to work offshore with impunity.

4. It is easy to send by post all manner of illegal articles—contraband, fake products (very dangerous if medicines or spare parts for cars), drugs, and even weapons—as the postal services do not have the means to screen effectively for these things.

5. Dishonest or fictitious businesses can divert their customer's electronic payment details for their own benefit, and hackers can steal them from the websites where they are stored since there is no cryptography that is unbreakable.

6. The means of combatting cybercrime are quite restricted. Most countries are not yet aware of the size of this crime problem even though the financial loss it causes has been huge for several years. A recent survey by the CSIS (Center for Strategic and International Studies) estimated that cybercrime and cyberespionage caused an annual loss of 100 billion dollars to the American economy and the loss of 508,000 jobs. The worldwide loss was estimated at 500 billion dollars.[97]

The Drug Market

The Internet facilitates drug consumption in many ways. It allows orders for drugs to be placed, or for the ingredients from which they can be cultivated or synthesized. The suppliers may be within the state or abroad, and the orders can be sent through the postal service with little fear of detection. It also provides recipes for making toxic substances oneself, and describes how cannabis and hallucinogenic mushrooms may be cultivated at home.

It also informs those who are interested of the development of new drugs, and how certain chemicals may be used as drugs.[98] It also helps to trivialize and spread the consumption of drugs through the exchange of experiences on forums.

The substances widely used by athletes to improve sporting performance should also be classed in the same category as drugs. In most countries these are forbidden by law, not only in the interests of fair play but also because they are dangerous. They are easily procured through the Internet from countries where they are tolerated by the law, or from underground suppliers.

All these transactions were and could still be possible without the Internet, but the Internet greatly facilitates them, aids them, and amplifies them.

Sectarian and Extremist Propaganda

The Internet has become the propaganda tool of choice for sects and groups of extremists who would get no hearing on mainstream media. Groups that would otherwise be obscure and unknown can easily present themselves to the public. Moreover, thanks to the ease with which people can be manipulated through texts, images, and especially videos[99] presented on the Internet, it is used to impress and recruit.

The sects have a strong Internet presence (more than 50,000 sites), and some of them use it to recruit, the Scientologists, the Jehovah's Witnesses and Soka Gakkai for instance. However, it has been even more useful to extremist political movements, which were formerly insignificant. They have greatly increased their membership and gained many sympathizers thanks to the way they have publicized their ideas, especially through talented bloggers.

Extremist religious movements have also greatly benefited by exploiting the advantages of the Internet as a tool for information and manipulation. It is common knowledge that the young people who have converted to Islam and joined the violent extremists like ISIS in the Middle East often did so under the influence of propaganda from certain Mosques and in the markets. But at least as many succumbed to the lure of their Internet sites that, as communication experts have noted, are run by past masters in the manipulation of minds. Their targets are often young people living in the countryside with no direct contact with Islamic extremes, but who are nonetheless convinced that they should join the jihad.

Suicide Pacts

Among the evil encounters lurking on the Internet and leading onto dangerous paths are those sites that promote suicide, which started to spread in the 1990s. Some of these sites have helped groups of young people to agree to commit mass suicide; others host the blogs of those sick with depression whose temptations to suicide tend to infect others of like mind; others describe the methods for ending one's life and attract especially those who seek euthanasia. The impact of these sick sites is certainly limited, but there is a clear correlation between their spread and the suicide rate of the young which can be observed the world over.[100]

Other sites that fall into the same category are those that promote anorexia, since this ailment is a subconscious expression of a death wish. Anorexia is of course a form of psychosis: a chronic mental illness which modifies one's perception of oneself and the world. It has deep roots in personal psychology and in family life, but it can blossom in a favorable environment. In adolescence, when teenagers feel ill at ease with their bodies, the media offer them skinny "top models" as role models of beauty and success. This influences the teenagers by encouraging them to imitate what they see, which was created by undernourishment and exaggerated by image retouching. They are drawn to start on a path that is dangerous for their health and even their lives.

CHAPTER 7

))

The Abolition of Private Life

Privacy is something which has emerged out of the urban boom coming from the industrial revolution; privacy may actually be an anomaly.
—Vint Cerf, chief evangelist at Google

If you have something that you don't want anyone to know, maybe you shouldn't be doing it in the first place.
—Eric Schmidt, CEO of Google

The new media have reduced the distinction between private and public life so much that in some cases it has completely disappeared. One cause of this is the deliberate and conscious action of the states and large companies that control big data. Another cause is the behavior, both conscious and unconscious, of individuals driven by certain psychological inclinations, which are encouraged by the way the new media work.

Reducing the Distance Between Public and Private Life

One of the most remarkable effects of the new media has been to help enormously the blurring of the boundaries between private and public life. Television, the Internet, and Facebook have been especially effective in this respect. Over 20 years ago, Lucien Sfez observed that modern communications meant "the end of the distinction between public and private which has been at the foundations of civil society and the state since the time of Christian Rome."[101]

In general, the television brings public life into the home, into what Hannah Arendt called "the security of private life,"[102] the intimate environment of the family, hitherto protected from intrusion. Its presence is more than intrusive. It is dominant. It takes the place of the mistress of the house for part of the day, which it organizes as a function of the programs, and it acquires more influence than the parents over the children.

It also gives private life a public dimension by multiplying "tele-reality" programs that aim to show people's private lives in the most intimate way. These programs transform the spectator into a voyeur. Any behavior that may attract attention is emphasized. This is often deviant behavior, or what corresponds to the passions of the spectators that they may or may not admit.

The television also insinuates itself into the family circles of politicians, or invites them to speak of their private lives on-screen. It is alleged that this will bring them closer to the people, but in fact, it merely deconsecrates their office and weakens their authority in modern society.

Virtually every computer is equipped with a small camera, or linked to one via Wi-Fi or Bluetooth. So, everyone can present themselves to the world in their most private and intimate environment. Some even go so far as to film themselves continuously, transmitting their every gesture, and every detail of their daily life.

Mobile phones can take photos and videos, and record sounds. This allows the words and behavior of people nearby to be recorded in secret, and then broadcast publicly through the Internet or Facebook. It has become impossible for well-known people, be they actors, singers, politicians, or anyone famous, to do, say, or react to anything anywhere at all without the risk of being recorded by someone and the result broadcast to the world at large.

In this field, as in others, the modern world is marked by a hatred of secrets and a culture of transparency. These arise not so much through love of truth, but in the service of exhibitionism and voyeurism, enabled by the new media that provide both the means and powerful encouragement for such behavior.

The Coming of Big Brother

All kinds of personal and confidential information transit through the new media and can be harvested to be stored for unlimited time. Many free Internet sites require users to provide some personal information in exchange for their service—age, address, telephone number, etc. Those who use Facebook are also required to reveal more private information—date and place of birth, schools and universities attended, their place of work, a list of their friends, their tastes in reading, music, and films, their main interests, photographs, etc. Sometimes users furnish such information to various sites naively or without thinking; sometimes they give them gladly to social networks, especially Facebook; and in all cases they are easily recovered by third parties.

Cambridge Analytica was a company specialized in strategic communication, which used tools to harvest and analyze data so as to provide political parties with a service that would influence opinion through the social media. Unbeknownst to 87 million users of Facebook, this company harvested all their personal data and used it to send them targeted messages to influence the way they voted in the American Presidential Elections. This scandal showed Facebook users how the company's software allowed all their most personal data to be synthesized and continuously updated in a database accessible to the company or its partners.

All the cards we use, be they bank cards, loyalty cards, or health service cards (Vitale in France), leave a trace that is recorded digitally every time they are inserted into a terminal. So, those who run the service have a mass of information about the users. Cameras mounted in public places observe us as we go by and record our movements, where we stop, what interests us, what we do, and whom we meet. Since the recordings are digital, they can easily be preserved for a long time. No communication between two persons can remain completely confidential. The emails and text messages transit through Internet service providers who have the technical means to scan them all and to record them. Under certain conditions, which become slacker with time, telephone calls can be recorded by the police or by espionage agencies at home or abroad. The location of computers, tablets, and mobile phones can be accurately determined, which allows their users' movements to be accurately tracked. Several suppliers of applications for smartphones link their functionality to the localization of their user. Google strongly encourages its users to provide their localization and has developed an application which memorizes all the different localizations entered and all the journeys between them. Another application, Google Driving, will predict the route to be taken as a function of the stored information!

In general one may say that the different Internet service providers who network the world have the technical capacity to locate in both space and time any user of a portable device connected to their network. Those with whom they communicate can be identified, revealing their relations, even when the content of the messages or conversations is not actually recorded. Comparing this information with the traces left by smart cards each time they are used allows, in principle, most of their daily journeys to be reconstituted, and even many of their activities too.

With a computer, it would be easy to analyze all this data and thus to deduce the habitual purchases of anyone, along with their cultural and economic levels and their state of health. Their daily activities, their usual haunts, their rare encounters, their tastes, their beliefs, their ideas, their desires, and their plans could also be evaluated. If, in addition, telephone conversations could be recorded along with tweets, text messages, and emails, it would be possible to know precisely everyone's ideas and a good part of their inner life.

By simply entering someone's name into a search engine such as Google much of his personal information can be found. Statistically, someone using the Internet leaves, willingly or unwillingly, an average of ten pieces of information on each site visited. Some of them are already recorded, which allows the search engine to suggest other sites to visit by using the browsing history of the client.

A computer capable of all this is under our noses. It is enough for our service provider to take control of the memory and disc storage of our personal computer for it to become a tool to control us through its access to every single one of our connections.

This is exactly what Microsoft does, by forcing the consent of the users of its systems; and with Apple, it owns the vast majority of the operating systems in the world. In the privacy statement, to which users of the latest version of Windows must agree, it is frightening to see how this American company collects the personal data of its users the world over.

Microsoft collects data to operate effectively and provide you the best experiences with our products. You provide some of this data directly, such as when you create a Microsoft account, administer your organization's licensing account, submit a search query to Bing, register for a Microsoft event, speak a voice command to Cortana, upload a document to OneDrive, purchase an MSDN subscription, sign up for Office 365 or contact us for support. We get some of it by recording how you interact with our products by, for example, using technologies like cookies, and receiving error reports or usage data from software running on your device.

"The data we collect depends on the context of your interactions with Microsoft, the choices you make, including your privacy settings, and the products and features you use. We collect data about the features you use, the items you purchase and the web pages you visit. This data includes your voice and text search queries or commands to Bing, Cortana and our chat bots. This also includes the settings you select and the software configurations you use most. [...] We collect data about your device and the network you use to connect to our products. It includes data about the operating systems and other software installed on your device, including product keys. It also includes IP address, device identifiers (such as the IMEI number for phones), regional and language settings. [...] We collect data about your interests and favorites, such as the teams you follow in a sports app, the programming languages you prefer, the stocks you track in a finance app or the favorite cities you add to a weather app. In addition to those you explicitly provide, your interests and favorites may also be inferred or derived from other data we collect. [...] We collect data about your contacts and relationships if you use a Microsoft product to manage contacts, for example Outlook.com, or to communicate or interact with other people or organizations, for example Visual Studio Team Services ...." In other words, they allow a complete user profile to be created for advertising purposes.[103]

The conditions of use for Cortana, the voice recognition software used by the system, are even more intrusive.

"To enable Cortana to provide personalized experiences and relevant suggestions, Microsoft collects and uses various types of data, such as your device location, data from your calendar, the apps you use, data from your emails and text messages, who you call, your contacts and how often you interact with them on your device. Cortana also learns about you by collecting data about how you use your device and other Microsoft services, such as your music, alarm settings, whether the lock screen is on, what you view and purchase, your browse and Bing search history, and more." […] "When you use OneDrive, we record the data concerning your use of this service as well as the content you save." But this is not all, as this piece of software also analyses undefined "speech data": "we collect your voice input, as well your name and nickname, your recent calendar events and the names of the people in your appointments, and information about your contacts including names and nicknames." […] "Microsoft does not use the content of your emails, discussions, video calls, voice mails, documents, photos or other personal files to send you targeted advertising [but it still uses] other information which we have collected over time using your demographic data your search requests, your centers of interest, your favorites, you user data and your localization data." […] "We will access, disclose and preserve personal data, including your content (such as the content of your emails, other private communications or files in private folders), when we have a good faith belief that doing so is necessary to," for example, "protect their customers" or "enforce the terms governing the use of the services." […] "The personal data collected by Microsoft may be recorded and analyzed in the United States of America or in any other country where Microsoft, its subsidiaries or service providers are present."

The personal data of Internet users are in fact collected by State agencies, such as the NSA, to control society, or by private corporations that sell, exchange, or exploit them for profit. The services provided by Google or Bing, which make on-line searching possible, and that allow vast numbers of documents (music, texts, videos, etc.) to be acquired free of charge only seem to be free. Behind the scenes there is a deal that brings great profit to the service providers at the expense of their clients. It is about this behavior that the proverb was coined: "When it's free, you're the product." This data does not pass away. It is harvested on a huge scale and stored indefinitely, thanks to the huge and infallible memories of the computers that handle it.

As Michel Bera and Eric Méchouan have shown, the Internet allows the creation of warehouses of data that allow individuals to be sorted, ranked, and filed away as never before.[104] So, as Alan Finkielkraut predicted: "The right to blot out the traces or to exist without leaving a trail will soon be gone. We will have gained many rights but will have lost the right to privacy."[105] The reign of Big Brother, described by George Orwell in his novel

1984, is no longer fiction. It can become reality by agreement between the different digital service providers, or by the creator of the dominant operating system accessing the memories of every computer that uses it, or by a state agency seizing data, legally or illegally. Indeed, it has already begun.

State Surveillance of Individuals

The United States and other advanced states have been able, for years, to observe and listen to individuals through satellite technology and to intercept telephone conversations and Internet traffic. This has allowed them to intercept electronic communications worldwide. Even heads of state are vulnerable to the NSA, as WikiLeaks has revealed. This agency has collaboration and sharing agreements with the large-scale harvesters of digital data,[106] particularly Google and Yahoo.[107]

Various state services can access this data: the police, the customs service, espionage agencies, and the tax authorities. Under the pretext of preventing terrorism, the French State recently gave its espionage agencies the right, unfettered by any supervision or control, to intrude into the private lives of all its citizens by the following means.

1. They can install "black boxes" on the telephone networks that allow the analysis of all their "metadata"[108] with an algorithm, which can be configured to capture what is desired. This is mass surveillance, since all the traffic is analyzed by the algorithm to detect automatically certain key words. The metadata seem harmless at first sight, since they do not directly reveal the content of the messages sent. But in fact, by cross-correlation, they allow the quick identification of the people involved,[109] and much private information about them to be obtained.
2. The use of key loggers, which allow every keystroke on the target's computer to be recorded.
3. The use of IMSI catchers, which can capture all telephone and Internet traffic within a radius of 500 meters.
4. Fitting cameras or microphones in a dwelling, or a GPS beacon to a vehicle.

Any citizen trying to escape the control of the state, by using encryption or by employing a program like Tor, becomes suspicious to state agencies as his identity, the IP address of his computer, and where he is are all hidden.

Suspicion is also aroused by an innocent visit to a site targeted by a surveillance algorithm. Equally suspicious is any person who makes contact with another who is already on a surveillance list.[110]

State or municipal surveillance systems are, of course, aimed at improving the security of the people; but they run up against the age-old problem that more liberty means less security and more security means less liberty. In this sphere, every democratic society has been obliged to compromise; but modern means favor overarching security. The insecurity felt by the citizens of modern societies, which arises from the way they have developed, encourages this. Morality has been weakened, mainly through loss of religious faith; delinquency and fanaticism, both religious and political, have increased; and the permeability of frontiers has been a boon to the mafia and organized crime. Overarching security requires better means of prevention, which in turn require ever better systems of surveillance to keep ahead of the means of evading them.

We have come, bit by bit, to a kind of totalitarianism that hides itself behind the invisibility of digital sensors. In an article published in *The Nation* (New York) on March 23, 2015, David Cole states:

> Imagine a state that compelled its citizens to inform it at all times of where they are, who they are with, what they are doing, who they are talking to, how they spend their time and money, and even what they are interested in. None of us would want to live there. Human-rights groups would condemn such a state for denying the most basic elements of human dignity and freedom. We'd pity its citizens for their inability to enjoy the rights and privileges we know are essential to a liberal democracy.
>
> In fact, this is the state in which we now live—with one minor wrinkle: the US government does not compel us directly to share any of the above intimate information with it. Instead, it relies on private companies to collect such information—and then it takes it from them at will.

If this form of totalitarianism that we now endure has arisen in a theoretically democratic state, we can imagine what it might be like in a hard-line totalitarian state that might develop from it, using all the above means of surveillance.

It is true that too much information drowns out information, that most of the information transmitted is of no interest, and that citizens who are above reproach have nothing to fear from being observed or overheard. But as Maurits Martijn and Rob Wijnbeerg have demonstrated in eleven points in their article in *De Correspondant* (Amsterdam), we all have something to hide: our intimate and personal life.

The possibility of being observed and overheard teaches us that nothing can be completely confidential. This is subjectively seen, and rightly so, as an intrusion into our private life, a violation of our intimacy, and an affront to human dignity.

Economic Control of Everyone

Many commercial organizations have agreed that from now on they will share and classify for profit all the personal data that they have acquired from the Internet through client registration, Internet searches and purchases, and loyalty cards. All this data is presently recorded, classified, and centralized in commercial data bases (Big Data). It is analyzed and further classified to establish customer profiles. The results of this *paneling*[111] can then be sold to other commercial organizations, which use them to target potential customers in client prospection software. One can easily see this on the main commercial sites on the web, such as Amazon. Simply searching for a product registers an interest that leads similar products to be proposed on subsequent visits to the site. In certain stores, there is an IT system that links to the mobile phone of every customer to record how much time is spent in front of each product. This gauge of customer interest allows commercial strategies to be developed.

Many websites, Google especially, nag users to register the location of their computers permanently. The location of a smartphone, with user permission, is recorded continuously, which can be obligatory with some applications. These locations are then used by commercial sites, or sold by dealers in big data, to allow commercial offers to be sent to customers from businesses in their area. Many of these offers succeed, since they are tuned to the passions, the desires, the interests, and the ease of access of the person targeted.

Official data concerning health services, such as the data on the Carte Vitale in France, are fairly well protected. But the various objects, such as bracelets and watches, connected to suppliers who are not subject to medical secrecy allow them to harvest data that can then be used for profit. For example, more and more people follow various bodily functions and activities. They track their movements and the number of paces taken all day long. They also record their weight, body mass, calorie intake and consumption, blood pressure and pulse rate, and monitor the rhythm, duration, and quality of their sleep. All this is recorded by applications on their smartphones or computers and transmitted to the service providers who have agreed to store them, synthesize them, and analyze them; but they also may easily exploit them. Google has recently proposed an application that allows Internet users to diagnose their illnesses from the symptoms that they enter into the search engine. It will then suggest non-prescription treatments. There is some profit to be made from the sale of medicines, but far more to be gained from commercializing all the information gathered on the health of those people who are naïve enough to provide this intimate and confidential data.

Different kinds of data allow service providers to make predictions that serve their own interests. Visa, one of the main providers of bank card services, is even able to calculate the risk of divorce by analyzing the pattern of their customers' purchases. Insurance companies are interested in harvesting data that helps them assess the risks of different customers. They look for information on their standard of living, employment stability and health, backed by health history and medical treatments, and also by eating habits and sporting activities. The same goes for banks when a loan is requested.

These are just a few examples of how the new media allow the economic control of individuals with a power never equaled before. For those who use big data, individuals are no more than data base entries of economic variables to be used for profit. They are numerical clones, each with an identity, but bereft of any humanity or personality.

Self-exposure and the Loss of Modesty and a Sense of Intimacy

The removal of the distance between private and public life is not simply due to the actions of states and large corporations that exploit big data. It is also caused by people themselves. The new media place them in a domain where it is easy to express and develop certain psychological and spiritual tendencies.

Following the work of Guy Debord,[112] many analysts have found that in different spheres, our society has become a "society of the spectacle" where a scenario is more important than reality and appearances are more important than being. It is a society oppressed by a real "tyranny of one's image."[113] Even those well placed in society, whose position is assured by their rank or their cultural and intellectual achievements, are subject to this. They use the new media to present themselves to the widest possible audience, driven by the new idea that the reality and value of what one has achieved is nothing if it is not known. It must be seen and discussed. One's fame is measured by the number of web pages where one is present, by the number of "friends" and "likes" on Facebook, or "followers" on Twitter.

The ease with which one may create a personal page, or a blog, on the Internet has encouraged people to expose themselves in every possible way. Facebook and Twitter encourage this still further so that anyone, even if of no account, can present himself more or less widely to the public to give the impression that he is well known.

Those who have nothing remarkable to offer try with all their might to make themselves noticed. One of the main ways of attracting attention is to present deviant or offensive behavior. Exposing one's psychological or physical intimacy will also serve to stimulate the voyeurism of potential spectators.

Everyone finds it easy to speak on the new media of personal matters that in former times were treated with discretion through self-respect, through modesty, or to avoid being shamed. This phenomenon shows how far the sense of intimacy has been lost, and how greatly the boundary between public and private life has been blurred. It is related to a loss of moral sense and to forgetfulness of what it means to be a person. For in each personality, including one's own, there are mysterious depths and a hidden identity.

Such behavior can also be seen in the way mobile phones are used everywhere in public spaces. The users speak loudly about all sorts of subjects without the least embarrassment or concern that they may be overheard by those next to them or may be intruding into other people's personal space.

The new media have not simply enabled self-exposure, but have encouraged over-exposure of oneself. One's intimacy is willingly or knowingly shown to the public at large. This "overexposed intimacy"[114] is called forth by the demand for total transparency in modern Western Societies and encouraged by the culture of narcissism that they have nurtured. As the American philosopher Christopher Lasch has shown, this culture of narcissism has invaded every section of society,[115] strongly supported by the new media.

In psychoanalysis, narcissism is classed as a form of "philautie," the ego-tistical love of oneself. Eastern Christian Spirituality considers this to be one of the basic passions of humanity, the mother of all the others. It has an extremely negative effect on the person as we will see in what follows.

CHAPTER 8

The Denial of the Body and Its Effects on Health

But if your eye is bad, your whole body will be full of darkness.
—Matthew 6:23

Setting Aside the Body

As we have seen above, when we looked at relationships between people, one of the effects of all the new media, without exception, has been to set aside the body. Apart from the organs of sense and the fingers which activate the keyboard, touchscreen, joystick, and remote control, the body is inactive, and to different degrees is isolated and absent, both from oneself and from others.

In all these situations, apart from the mobile phone, *homo connecticus* is immobile on a chair, forgetting his body. In general, he cuts himself off from others to concentrate on his screen; and if he does relate to others, it is most often without his body.

Placing one's body out of sight and being blind to the bodies of others are not caused only by the media. It also is due to the desire to escape and hide out of sight of others so as not to face up to their real existence to which the physical presence of their bodies bears witness. Thus many people are more at ease communicating when their bodies cannot be seen and they are not face to face. They do not realize that this flight from themselves and from the bodily presence of others is the sign of a neurotic attitude.

Isaac Asimov predicted this disembodied culture in his novel, *The Naked Sun*. The inhabitants of the planet Solaria were glued to their computers in their homes and had no physical relationship with each other. Were they to encounter bodily another individual, they became tense and panicked. Philippe Breton asks: "Does not this new cult of the virtual deny the body as the root of man's identity, as David Le Breton has demonstrated and strongly denounced?"[116] Le Breton observes that in general, "A religion of the machine imposes itself on a background of the denigration of man and contempt for his inherent bodily nature."[117] He shows how for those who use the new media their bodies become a burden, which hinders their activity with their physical needs; and also, through the play of perversion and makeovers, become broken beings whose identity is blurred:

> Navigating the internet or virtual reality gives people the impression that they are burdened by a body to which they are chained. It must be fed, cared for and maintained, and life without it would be much happier, free from those troubles. Faceless and bodiless communication encourages multiple identities, and the disintegration of the person, who is consumed by a flow of encounters in each of which a different identity is assumed. The name, age, sex and profession are chosen to suit the circumstances. Cyber-culture is often described by those who embrace it as a world of wonders, where mutants invent a new universe which is, of necessity, a bodiless paradise.[118]

The New Media as a Health Risk

The negative effects of the new media on health have led two American pediatricians to the following conclusion, which applies also to adults: "The media should be recognized as a major public health problem."[119] In his book, *TV Lobotomie. La vérité scientifique sur les effets de la télévision*, Michel Desmurget emphasizes how much damage the television can do to the body. Here is the introduction to his chapter "La télé, menace de la santé":

> Imagine a recreational substance whose consumption would increase considerably the incidence of obesity, smoking, alcoholism, sleep disorders, attempted suicides, dangerous sexual habits and eating disorders (anorexia and bulimia). Would you accept this substance in your home? Would you allow your children to use it? I don't

think so! If I am not mistaken about this, then it is clear that the vast majority of television watchers and responsible parents are not aware of the poisonous effects of the small screen. There are dozens of scientific studies which show with frightening consistency that there is no difference at all between the effects of this imaginary substance and of the television. The television is not a source of harmless amusement. It is a major health hazard.[120]

Reduction of Physical Activity

The unhealthy effects on the body of the new media are caused first by the considerable reduction of physical activity that results when one spends several hours per day motionless in front of a screen. The bad effects of a sedentary lifestyle are well documented in medical journals; and with the growth of the service industries over recent decades, there has been a big reduction in physical activity in many jobs, which is only partially compensated by sporting activity.

There is abundant evidence from many studies that the time spent watching television is correlated to an increased risk of cardio-vascular problems.[121] The results may be extended to other media—video games and the Internet for instance—which involve remaining almost motionless in front of a screen for long periods.

Staring at a screen with motionless eyelids for long periods causes various ocular problems. The eyes become dry and irritated, which can cause problems of focusing and mental fatigue as one strains to compensate.

The development of domestic appliances and e-commerce also reduces physical activity in a way that harms health. The first reduces or eliminates for the habitually inactive even the light activity of household chores that might have improved their body tone. The second removes the need to go out and walk around the shops. Home entertainment from television and Internet has the same immobilizing effect.

Debasement of Eating Habits, Bulimia, and Obesity

Screen time, be it television, video games, or Internet, has unfortunate effects upon eating habits: meals are taken at irregular times and fast food is consumed, all so as to lose as little screen time as possible. Meals are not properly cooked and diet is not balanced. Watching television encourages the nibbling of high-calorie snacks (pop-corn, crisps, biscuits, cakes, etc.) that, statistically, takes place for about 15% of the time in front of the screen. High-calorie drinks are also consumed, sugary sodas by the children and beer or other alcoholic drinks by adults and even adolescents. All this adds up to a mechanical, and so unconscious, bulimia. One of its effects is obesity, which is also a result of inactivity. Of course, too much screen time is not the only cause of obesity, but it helps greatly, and one may say: "The more time you spend in front of the screen, the more likely you are to be fat."[122]

The factors mentioned above[123] have their greatest effect on childhood obesity. They affect adults insofar as the adults stick to the bad habits picked up earlier, which increase fatness. Many health problems arise from this: high blood pressure, the risk of a stroke, diabetes, arthrosis, hypercholesterolemia, sleep apnea, problems with the endocrine gland, and certain cancers. Psychological problems arise as well, related to low self-esteem. Overall, obesity increases mortality rates by 50% to 80%.[124]

Alcoholism and Addiction to Tobacco

In his book, *TV Lobotomie. La vérité scientifique sur les effets de la télévision*, Michel Desmurget studies in depth how one becomes alcoholic[125] or addicted to tobacco,[126] both of which, of course, have grave effects upon health. Both are encouraged by the television in two different ways. For a start, your passive attitude as you watch television encourages smoking and drinking. This, like nibbling, is largely automatic and unconscious. Also, the television companies advertise alcohol and cigarettes. This has a big impact on adolescents and forms habits, which they maintain as they grow up. In some countries, those of the European Union for instance, advertising is prohibited for tobacco, and tightly controlled for alcohol. However, some of the movies and soap operas screened encourage their consumption by trivializing it.[127] They depict characters, whom the young will see as heroes or role models, smoking and drinking. They are meant to be seen as models of virility and social success to be imitated; and when programs such as a football match are watched by a group, all the members generally drink.

American research has shown that every hour adolescents spend watching television increases by about 10% the probability that they will become regular drinkers within 18 months.[128] As regards tobacco, research on children of between 9 and 12 years old has shown that 35% of them began to smoke through the examples they were given in movies and soap operas.[129] Further research on children of between 10 and 14 years old, whose parents did not smoke, showed that 52% of them had begun to smoke through this influence.[130]

We will dwell no longer on this subject since it is specific to television and to those media that show movies and soap operas. There are other media to consider that do not leave the hands free for eating, smoking, and drinking, and are not conditioned so much by advertising.

Sleep Problems

One of the most obvious effects of the use of the new media on the body is sleep deprivation with all the psychological problems that come with it. The clinical sleep problems related to the new media are associated with a reduction of the time asleep below what is normal for a particular age group. This is not necessarily due to addiction, but may simply be caused by the need to view a late-night program to the end, the need to consult the Internet late at night, or the need to finish off email and SMS correspondence. Worse problems may arise when there is a degree of addiction. For example, online chats or video games may lead some young people to stay awake all night, with serious effects on the next day's activities, at work or at college.

Problems of sleep quality affect most active users of the new media, especially with screens. They include problems with going to sleep and waking up often during the night with difficulty going back to sleep. The result is tiredness upon waking in the morning, which continues throughout the day. These problems have various causes. First of all, it is well known that sleep consists of a series of cycles. When the beginning of the first cycle is a failure and doesn't lead to sleep, it is transferred to the second cycle. This failure of sleep cycles is due to the normal physiological mechanisms that induce sleep being supplanted by something stronger: the end of a television film, or the end of Internet and social network activities.

A second, and natural, cause of the problem is that going to sleep is linked to a decrease of light intensity. Watching a computer screen counteracts this process and helps to keep the Internet user awake. This is less true for watching the television, where the viewer is related less closely to the screen.

A third cause is that an active relationship with the new media (with computers more than the television) keeps the attention alert and all of one's faculties awake.

A fourth cause is that the way the content of the Internet is always changing, discontinuously and without structure, produces a certain disorder in the mind. This leads to troubled sleep and disturbs the moments of wakefulness which, in turn, hinder going back to sleep.

A fifth cause may be the content itself. If it contains scenes that arouse our emotions or shake our sensitivities, it can be disturbing, especially for children. Michel Desmurget writes: "the more a child watches television, the greater the risk of troubled nights. Some of the symptoms are parasomnia, screams of anguish, problems of going to sleep, refusal to go to bed, nightmares and frequent awakening at night."[131]

Tiredness and Stress

A reduction in the time or quality of sleep brings on tiredness. This adds to the psychological and mental fatigue linked to the use of the new media (of which we will speak later) and impacts the body. It leads to a state of debility if the body is not toned up with physical work or sport. Moreover, the body itself is stressed by using the new media leading to various physiological problems.

CHAPTER 9

The Dominance of the Virtual over the Real

Our age prefers the image to the object, a copy to the original, a depiction to the reality, the superficial to being .... What is sacred for this age is illusion, and the profane is seen as truth.

—Feuerbach, The Essence of Christianity

When ghosts become real, reality becomes ghostly.

—Gunter Anders, The Obsolescence of Man

The main characteristic of the new media is that in what they broadcast and in the relationships they create they bring about a virtual reality. It mirrors reality, and gradually becomes more and more important until reality is completely swamped. In the mind of *homo connecticus*, the image he has of the world has become more important than the world itself.

Pride of Place for the Image

A great change has been brought about by the new media in the way people see the world: the image has become all important. This change started many decades ago in the printed media, newspapers, weekly magazines, and periodicals. They published more and more photographs, ever more striking and even shocking, and this gave rise to the famous advertising slogan of a well-known French weekly: "The weight of the words; the punch of the picture."

At the same time, the image has acquired a place of growing importance in daily life. It is the main tool of advertising that has penetrated all the media and marks our environment with its billboards both in towns and along country roads. It is the main characteristic of the television that has invaded every home. Subsequently it has taken pride of place in all the new media, be they the Internet the social networks or the MMS, everything enabled by computers, tablets, and smartphones.

Much has been written about the special power of the image, and how it can convey a message more easily and powerfully than mere words. This special power is due mainly to two factors: first, it is perceived by the eye, which is the most sensitive and receptive of all the organs of sense; and second, it has a special power to arouse the emotions, sentiments, and attachments and to incite desire or repulsion. As Pascal said, long before there were specialists in communication, the power to convince depends less on the reason than on the imagination and sensitivity,[132] and a touching image is far more convincing than a well-thought-out and well-presented argument.

Advertisers understood from the start the profit they could gain through the power of images. The media use them too, to increase the number of their readers and spectators. And so have various other organizations whose interest is to steer public opinion and to manipulate the masses.

The power of an image to provoke action or reaction can be enhanced by tuning it to produce the desired results. The exact moment a photograph is taken and its angle of view can influence strongly the way what it records will be seen. So can the choice of particular people or moments as subjects during the unfolding of a complex event. In a documentary film, the script allows the shots and the people filmed to be chosen in advance, and subsequent editing allows certain scenes to be retained and others removed so as to slant the information as desired. Image enhancement software, such as Photoshop, allows images to be altered at will to be more attractive or more repulsive. Parts of the image can be airbrushed away, removing some of the people present or changing the background. In all these ways a certain view can be imposed of what took place and the roles of various people, along with the corresponding emotions, sentiments, desires, and opinions.

However, it is not only in these media that the image is treated as more important than the reality it is supposed to represent. The same thing occurs in the daily life of all those immersed in digital devices. It is so easy for anyone to take a photograph that they have proliferated in daily life. There are so many ways this can be done: with digital cameras, tablets, and especially smartphones, which are so easy to use. They are light, handy, and cheap, for the photos cost nothing. In addition to the selfies he takes in a mad desire to multiply pictures of himself, *homo connecticus* feels the need to photograph every situation in which he finds himself. The moment of life, the people with him, the nature which surrounds him, or even the dish he is eating, all have less importance for him than the digital images he takes of them. This photographic bulimia is quite unlike the photographs of former times. They were printed on paper and stuck into an album so that they could be consulted later by the family to remind them of joyful and memorable events in the past. The number of digital photos is so inflated that there is no time to consult them even when they are saved onto a dedicated drive. On the photographic device, they must be periodically deleted to make room for more. They are often intended for sharing on Facebook, but the "friends" or "followers," drowned by a flood of images from everywhere,[133] ensure that their life is brief.

What is most worrying is that it is more important to have taken the photo and to have shared it on Facebook or Twitter than to have felt and experienced the event. People photograph a landscape without first taking the time to contemplate it, and once the picture is taken it becomes the main thing, giving them the impression that the landscape is their own. The digital photographer experiences reality only through its representation and its permanent transmission. He becomes separated from reality and plunges into a world of ghosts.

By giving *homo connecticus* the ability to copy the world, the new media dull his desire to discover it and to experience it in reality. While claiming to enrich his life, in fact they impoverish it. They limit his field of action while claiming to enlarge it. Does he really wish to explore far-off lands with all the expense, fatigue, and danger that this implies when the films he can watch on the Internet or the television place these lands opposite his armchair? Does he really wish to travel and queue at a museum when Google gives him Art Project that shows him high-resolution images of 40,000 great works from museums worldwide at the click of a mouse? It is here that we see clearly the trickery of it all. The size of the pictures and their original colors are absent. It is not possible to view them from different distances and angles the better to appreciate them. Above all, the emotion linked to seeing them in a place specially designed for viewing them is impossible. Instead of viewing the originals in a museum, the spectator sees a group (or series) of copies, rather like the work of a forger, but diminished by being reduced to the size of the screen, and to two dimensions in the case of sculptures.

The Dominance of the Virtual over the Real

The ease with which images can be created, manipulated, and transmitted, and the importance they have attained has allowed the new media to set up a virtual world in parallel to the real and more forceful than it. This situation could be foreseen 40 years ago by those who had thought carefully about the media. Among them was Guy Debord who wrote *La societé du spectacle*. It begins with this remark: "The whole life of societies in which modern conditions of production prevail may be seen as a vast mass of scenarios. Any living experience is set at a distance by the way it is presented."[134] This spectacle, or representation of the world which parallels it and ends up by replacing it, consists mainly of images: "The spectacle cannot be considered simply as an abuse of the visible and a result of the techniques of massive image transmission. It is more a *Weltanschauung*[135] which has come to life and been materialized. It is a vision of the world which has become objectivized."[136] This unreal world of the spectacle is not neutral, but overall reflects the orientation of society. In the modern Western World its end is essentially in politics, and even more in economics, for in this world, politics is dominated by economics.

> The spectacle, taken as a whole, is both the result and the source of the existing style of production. It is not an addition to the real world, stuck on like a decoration. It is the unreal heart of real society. In all its various forms, news or propaganda, advertising or direct consumption of amusements, the spectacle is the present model of the dominant life of society. It is the ever-present affirmation of the choice already made in production and in the consumption which goes with it. The form and content of the spectacle are the complete justification of both the conditions and the aims of the existing system.[137]

The society of the spectacle, says Debord, is in an unreal state, consisting of appearances, which denies reality and real life: "Considered on its own terms, the spectacle is the assertion of appearances, and the claim that all human and social life consists simply of appearances; but the criticism which reaches the truth of the spectacle reveals it to be the visible denial of life; or a denial of life which has become visible."[138] The spectacle thus becomes a kind of ideal and moral norm: "The spectacle presents itself as hugely positive, unchallenged and inaccessible. All which remains is this: what appears is good, and what is good appears."[139] The society of the spectacle creates a double illusion: it presents as unreal what is real, and as real what is unreal: "Where the real world is transformed into mere images, mere images become real and the effective drivers of hypnotized behavior."[140] Debord's criticism belongs to Marxist thought and is heavily influenced by Feuerbach. It is limited by its confinement to the economic realm, which is well expressed by the axiom: "The root of the spectacle is in the realm of the economy of abundance."[141] Modern media, however, substitute a representation (mainly with images) of reality for reality itself in all spheres of society, economic, political, religious, etc. They also extend it to the individual sphere. They facilitate the representation and staging of oneself, and the creation of a character, in parallel with one's real self, to replace the real person.

The television has greatly helped to set up a world where reality is seen as a spectacle and where spectacles are created to be passed off as realities.[142] Generally, the television distances the spectator from reality even as it claims to depict it, for, as Liliane Lurçat remarks: "It is not the world, but a mirage of the world depicted in images."[143] We never reach the world through the television. Instead, we reach a substitute.[144] The problem lies in the image and in its power. It makes it seem as though our eyes see reality directly and perceive its nature. It gives the spectator the false impression that he has reality before his eyes. As Liliane Lurçat writes: "Relating to reality through the media fosters a habit of belief, rather than the desire to analyze and understand. The image is the bearer of its own credibility and has no need to refer to any external reality."[145]

It is not only the popular tele-reality programs, with their scenes staged in advance and edited before viewing, that are responsible for this. News programs, one might think, should be more serious; but the way they are produced also tends to present reality as a spectacle. Not only do they emphasize the most spectacular events that may not be specially important or significant, they also rely on movie production techniques. Sometimes they are faked, the better to manipulate opinion especially in the political sphere. Sometimes events are invented, or a pseudo-event, like an advertising launch, is given more emphasis than real events. In every case the events are distorted when reported and are either amplified or minimized. The search for the novel and spectacular often removes the important events of yesterday from sight, because new events have occurred that will stimulate anew the blunted attention of the spectators. All these questions have been carefully analyzed, using examples, by Ignacio Ramonet in his essay *La Tyrannie de la communication*.[146]

Liliane Lurçat has studied the effects of the unrealistic qualities of the television on the education of children:

> Though the television brings the world into the home, it does so unrealistically, for a link to reality implies activity, the participation of the five senses and handling things. [...] On the television screen, true life is absent as Arthur Rimbaud has said. [...]. The time spent watching television is taken from other activities which, though humble, are in touch with reality and with other people. Children may go to the market, make contact with other people, pursue DIY, improvise solutions etc. In all these circumstances the children develop through active contact and interaction with others. Their personalities are forged and they become members of society. If these activities are absent, children may sink beneath an overdose of television. They are cut off from reality and live enclosed in a televisual world.[147]

The same author also remarks:

> The television also cuts us off from reality since everything it shows, be it fiction or fact, is transposed into images. This leads to problems with distinguishing and discriminating since in childhood, we have difficulty distinguishing the real from the imaginary.[148]

Apart from the television, all the new media create their own virtual worlds. Video games are clearly a special case. They create a multitude of obviously virtual sub-worlds inspired by comic strips, science fiction, or fantasy literature that describes imaginary wonders, often in an imaginary past and in imaginary lands.

There is also the Internet, which is a whole world in itself. This is cyberspace that William Gibson described in his novel *Neuromancer* as "a consensual hallucination experienced daily by billions of legitimate operators, in every nation."[149] The users of the web are not only disconnected from their real immediate environment, but also plunged into a multifaceted world of fabricated sites where they are drawn by their links onto "the information highways."

The social networks and discussion forums also give rise to parallel worlds that are in large measure virtual and dematerialized. Bodies are absent, and there is much that is fake or artificial. In these worlds, it is rare to find someone who goes under a true identity. The discussion forums are frequented by people who hide behind pseudonyms. When they are not playing a role, they present themselves in the most favorable light, which may bear no relation to their true reality.

According to Lucien Sfez, the main result of the development of such communication is the confusion of the fact with its representation, especially by the media. This leads to the growth of a specific social pathology that he calls tautism. This is a combination of tautology and autism that encloses people in a maze of representations from which there is no exit. It simply turns people back on themselves.[150]

"The tautistic phenomenon," writes Sfez, can be described thus: "what is real is no longer taken to be represented. Reality is no longer what has been invented expressed by its name. Tautism takes the represented reality for an expressed reality. What is represented is taken to be what represents. The second degree realities produced by transmitters, and the third degree realities produced by receivers are taken to be one and the same first degree reality and are confused with basic facts. It is as though these were basic facts, and the whole chain of intermediaries which had extracted the information, set it in context and brought it to the receiver had suddenly been removed. It is as if the receiver itself was nothing but an absorbent sponge which accepted any transmitted electrical signal. This is the totalitarianism of tautism, a dumb folly which denigrates reality, an all-embracing aim closed in on itself as Baudrillard described.[151] [...] Tautism, let us say, is the contraction of two terms, autism and tautology. Autism is the sickness of self-enclosure where the individual feels no need to express his thoughts to others or to conform to the thoughts of others. Its sole aim is organic or pleasurable satisfaction."[152]

The fact that people "henceforth take a represented reality for an expressed reality" is for Sfez "the fundamental confusion, the source of delirium."[153]

Virtual Reality and Augmented Reality: Two New Products on the Drug Market

Over the last few years, the IT industry has developed headsets[154] that allow their users to be immersed in an artificial virtual reality. All the senses are involved, sight, hearing, smell, and touch. Sound comes from different places and images are 3-D. Odors are diffused and the body feels movements and impulses to which it can react. These devices cut their users off from their environment so much that they lose touch with its existence. They are plunged into a world that is either completely imaginary, or where reality is augmented by being combined or overlaid with unreal effects. In his work *The Metaphysics of Virtual Reality*,[155] Michael R. Heim distinguishes its seven characteristics: simulation, interaction, the artificial, immersion, tele-presence, total bodily immersion, and communication through the net.

As usual, the creators emphasize the advantages of these methods for culture and learning, but it is obvious that as inheritors of the realistic video game, they share its characteristics. They allow one to evade the real world and forget its sorrows, difficulties, failures, and inconvenience by being immersed in a world that has none of these things, but instead fulfils all one's desires. In this way they do better than alcohol or drugs, that, although they help us to forget the world and ourselves by blurring our consciousness, fail to give even the appearance of a solution to our problems. They neither promise us what we do not have (augmented reality) nor do they propose an imaginary world in which to hide (complete virtual reality).

Of course, just as spirit merchants remain sober, and drug traffickers abstain from drugs for commercial reasons, the providers of virtual reality steer clear of their product. A photo taken at the opening of the Mobile World Congress in Barcelona in 2016 illustrates this and was widely circulated. It shows Mark Zuckerberg, the founder of Facebook, striding bare headed and radiant toward a room full of spectators wearing headsets. They all looked like cyborgs, staring straight ahead at a reality that does not exist, totally unaware of each other, and of the king of their world, striding toward them and savoring his power.[156]

A New Application of the Allegory of the Cave

It is amazing to see how today's world brings forth what Plato described, four centuries before our era. People live side by side yet do not see each other. Instead, from their earliest childhood they are glued to their screens, fascinated by the artificial objects that move and the sounds they make. It illustrates perfectly the allegory of the cave, the subject of a dialogue between Socrates and Glaucon:

> Now, represent to yourself in the way I shall describe the state of our nature as regards learning and ignorance. Imagine men who dwell beneath the earth in a cave with its entire mouth open to the light. From their childhood, these men have their legs and necks bound so that they cannot move or see anything except what is before them since their bonds prevent them turning their heads. The light comes from a fire burning on high at a great distance behind them. Between the prisoners and the fire there is a road set above them. Imagine that all along this road a little wall has been built, like the screens which puppet masters place before them and above which they show their wonders.
>
> I see that, said he.
>
> Now suppose that along that road pass men carrying objects which project above the wall, statuettes of men and animals, in stone in wood and every kind of material. Naturally some of these men speak, and others are silent.
>
> What a strange picture, he cried, and what strange prisoners.
>
> They are like us, I replied. First of all, do you think that in such a position they have ever seen anything of themselves or their neighbors except their shadows thrown by the fire on the cave wall in front of them?
>
> How can it be otherwise? He observed, if they are forced to keep their heads motionless their whole life long?
>
> And for the objects which pass by, is it not the same?
>
> Certainly.
>
> So if they could discuss things amongst themselves, would they not take the shadows which they see for real objects?
>
> It cannot be otherwise.[57]

In this passage, Plato denounced the estrangement of the sensible world in which he saw a shadow of the intelligible world. But the virtual world is an estrangement to the power of 2 since it gives us simply the shadow of a shadow.

CHAPTER 10

☜

Mental Disorders

I am troubled, I am bowed down greatly; I go mourning all the day long.

—Psalm 38:6 (NKJV)

The way the new media are used nowadays is a way that touches on the area of mental disorders. These may be mild or severe with strong links to neuroses, such as obsessions, anxiety, compulsive behavior, and problems of interpersonal relations. It also touches on the psychotic, through life in a world parallel to the real world, through changes in the way the world and others are seen, through narcissism, and through autism.

Obsessional and Compulsive Behavior

One of the most evident forms of pathological behavior is the obsessional and compulsive (frequent, repeated, impulsive, and unbridled) use of certain media. This is particularly so with the smartphone and computer, used in general for consulting one's inbox and social media accounts, or for sending messages and tweets, or to post items to a Facebook account, or to play with applications, or to consult the Internet about every idle thought that passes through the mind, or to telephone with nothing important to say, or to take photos of anything at all in any situation, or to buy things online without really needing them (the new media use such habits to feed other compulsions), or to change continuously the television channel. The remote control is the ancestor of the keyboard, and zapping the first example of this kind of compulsion.

The Fears and Anxiety Aroused by Hyperconnectivity

Hyper-connectivity and hyper-connection both serve to arouse fear and anxiety, linked to solitude and the feeling of loneliness. The first means being permanently connected to one or several media so as to be in contact. The second means being effectively in contact very frequently through the same media. Hyper-connectivity also tends to arouse anxiety and the fear[158] of getting lost, or to lose physically those close to one in a society perceived as ever more dangerous and menacing.[159] This leads parents to give their children a mobile phone as soon as they are able to go out alone so that they can be contacted, or make contact, at any time. This comforts their belief that the link is always there. Sometimes parental anxiety even reaches the level of paranoia, and they install active GPS on their children's smartphones so as to follow continuously their geographical location and their movements.

The new media also arouse anxiety through fears of losing oneself (psychologically or intellectually) in a society that gets more and more complex, and where the new media, as we have seen, have often become indispensable for getting one's bearings or for fulfilling certain needs or social requirements. The Internet can fill this need, but even more it is filled by smartphones that connect to the Internet and also provide emails, text messages, and interpersonal voice communication. For modern man the social media have also become necessities of life, which give him worth in the eyes of others. Their absence fills him with the fear of being diminished and despised in his very being. The psychiatrists Michel Hautefeuille and Dan Véléa describe thus the anguish that grips the addicts of the new technology when they lose their instrument:

> Of all the addictions to the new technologies it is the addiction to the mobile phone, tablet or phablet which has appeared in the most explosive fashion, not only amongst the young, but also amongst those of more advanced years. The development of these phones has enabled them to function as internet terminals. The addiction is growing ever stronger and is shown by the fear and panic which grip the users when they are separated from their phones. This fear has

been called "nomophobia," a contraction of *no mobile phone phobia*. Amongst the patterns of behavior of these new addicts, one typically finds impulsiveness and intolerance of frustration, but also a need for a display of social status. The loss of the device, whether misplaced, lost or stolen, is felt to be a blow to the identity and is combined with a feeling of abandonment, loneliness and vulnerability.[160]

A False Solution to Anxious Feelings and the Need for Reassurance

Adolescents rarely switch off their phones and even place them against their bodies so that they can feel them vibrate. They keep them by their side all night long and have the reflex of consulting them at any available moment,[161] not only when lessons are over, but also secretly, during their lessons. The mobile phone seems to have replaced the comforter, or teddy bear, which small children clasp tightly and look at, like a reassuring friend.

Adults themselves also place their phones next to their bodies. They constantly check that it is in their pocket or their handbag. They constantly glance at it wherever they may be to make sure that they have not received any new message, and when there is nothing, they check that their phone is still working and properly charged. The phone thus becomes the source of new disquiet, but its possession is itself the result of a certain disquiet and the need for reassurance when thus troubled.

It is important for parents to be able to locate their offspring through their phones; but it also seems to be reassuring for everyone who possesses a mobile phone to know that they can be located and called at any time. Otherwise they could feel lost in the vast world, exposed to its risks and at risk of missing some important event. This desire for permanent contact is clearly linked to the fear of solitude. It is a way of escape from the anxiety that this fear causes in a world where human relationships are strained, and for some are rare, or even totally absent.

This need for permanent contact is also linked to an inability to face oneself and to bear those moments of solitude, which are part of personal existence.[162] It reveals one as unable to live through those moments alone with oneself that are needed to fashion the person, to stabilize one's psychology, and to develop and deepen the spiritual life.

When parents become pathologically possessive and wish not only to locate their children but also to watch them closely through applications linking their smartphones, they deprive them totally of the minimum feeling of freedom they need. And they also teach them to see the world as a hostile and menacing place that must be approached with fear. They transfer their own anxiety to their young ones and fail to show them how to become independent. They give them no help to face the unknown or unexpected by marshaling their own resources, and they keep them in a state of dependency that stops them growing up.

Through his need of permanent contact, connected man "ties a leash to his foot" and makes of the World Wide Web a spider's web in which he shuts himself up.

A Means of Escaping Boredom

The success of the new media, especially the Internet and the social media, to which the computer and smartphone give access, is due in large measure to the way they counteract boredom. They allow the void that modern man feels in himself to be filled. His inner life has been greatly impoverished by its lack of a spiritual dimension, and his social life is diminished by the weakening of contacts with those around him, with his spouse, his family, his friends, and with society in general. It is true that one can contact them all the time, and be contacted as well. Even the shortest period of waiting time or inactivity can be eliminated at once. The least time of latency of the mind can be avoided, for the media offer the means of attracting the attention and stimulating the mind continuously. The Internet and the mobile phone are ways of passing the time when one is prevented from, or incapable of, passing it otherwise. They are means of filling the empty spaces in our lives, which can be huge for those who do not study or have a job or take part in sports or cultural activities. They are ways of warding off the anxiety born of a life that is empty, or has little to offer.

They push away boredom not just by filling the time but also by the novelties they show. These are not just fresh pieces of news. They are also things formerly unknown that can be discovered at any time and as much as desired through following links to different sites.

As regards boredom, the new media are mental regulators that avoid, or rather bypass, depression by a continual headlong rush to novelty. They are also social regulators, and as such are strongly encouraged by States and institutions. As Michel Hautefeuille and Dan Véléa remark: "Boredom is probably the worst enemy of social tranquility [...] Boredom in society serves to bottle up an energy of bitterness and despair which can only be released in violence unless it is regulated by effective social dampers."[163] In many ways the new media act as such dampers:

— Their constant technological innovation is always providing something new that is able to dissipate the boredom of modern man when faced with a dull world or one which repeats itself.
— They give a person, enclosed in an ever more restricted world, the illusion of individual freedom and mastery. They encourage the feeling that at every moment one has unlimited access to all possible information and that one can express oneself anywhere, just as the user of a smartphone can imagine that he transcends all limitations of the space where he lives.
— They offer an outlet for various impulses, passions, or fantasies, especially through games, images, videos, and movies. In this way they reduce the risk of mental instability or undesirable social behavior.
— They bring into the home a host of amusements that allow the real world to be forgotten with all its difficulties. They facilitate diversions in the sense Pascal gave to this word: they turn one's attention from one's own existential poverty and the anguish that it arouses.

A Distorted Vision of the World

As we have already remarked, one of the problems caused by the new media is that they make their users live in a virtual world, in parallel to the real world. The more time they spend with the media, and the more they concentrate on them, the more they are affected. This virtual world may be partly imaginary, or entirely as with television dramas or video games. It is not always completely unreal, but in every case, its reality is diminished, for example by the physical absence of other people on the Internet or in phone conversations. It is often deformed, just as an image can be a distortion of what it represents. It is often fraudulent as a result of the manipulations facilitated by all the new media.

Because of this, the representation of the world that is acquired through the new media has a psychotic character. For psychoses are mental illnesses whose symptom is delirium, that is, a representation of reality deformed by a partly imaginary interpretation. In extreme cases, which are rare, the boundary between the real and the imaginary becomes so blurred that the imaginary is believed to have been part of life, and real events are handled in ways inspired by the imaginary, as if it were part of real life. This behavior is generally found in those who watch movies and soap operas a great deal and spend much time playing video games. This sometimes leads to fantasies being acted out in real life, for example those that are violent or sexual.

In the best case, the world is seen and judged by the standards of the movies and soap operas. These strive to retain the interest of the audience by showing marginal, extreme, or deviant behavior. At the same time, they trivialize this behavior so as to make it seem normal or normative. All this has a powerful influence on the way viewers and Internet users see the world and ethical standards and on how they behave in reality.

Another of the milder but significant influences of the new means of communication is a reduction of the quality of interpersonal relationships. This affects the psychology of their users in their approach to others, and on how they handle their relationships with others that, as we have already seen, have become more abstract and impoverished.

The Image and Representation of Oneself as More Important Than Reality

The Internet and social media have also greatly changed the relationships of individuals with themselves. Existential philosophy, such as that of Sartre and the personalist philosophy that is linked with it, have strongly emphasized that, for the individual, the idea of "for another" (what he seems to be in the eyes of another) is fundamental to his consciousness of his existence, his identity, and his worth. The Internet and the social media allow everyone access to vast new means of social self-representation. But also, through various technical contrivances, they allow one to stage oneself in a flattering and exaggerated way.

In traditional societies, the person had little social value. Either the community or the collectivity eclipsed him, or his ethical values, such as the humility and modesty encouraged by Christianity, led him to self-effacement. The people who were specially valued in former times were heroes or creators, those whose action had a real impact on the preservation of society or its development in different fields. The Renaissance and the centuries that followed it valued the individuality of the artist, not only for his creativity but also for his originality. The traditional media of the twentieth century gave greater importance to all those involved in political life and social progress. In all these cases, social value was linked to a real social contribution and its recognition by society. It depended on the collectivity and not on the individual.

The new media allow you to photograph yourself, to video yourself, and to record yourself. Furthermore, they allow all these representations of yourself to be edited with various applications and to be posted on various social media, such as Facebook, or on Internet sites dedicated to their transmission, like YouTube for videos.

Anything goes if it will set you apart from the rest, be it fringe, eccentric, extreme, or dangerous. You can be a hero for a day by making a record-size pizza, by driving a car at 125 mph down a city street or by downing several bottles of spirits, one after the other. Provocative tweets or short, cutting phrases on blogs, Facebook, or Twitter are also ways to make yourself heard, to create a buzz, and to make people speak about you, even in political circles.

Getting others to speak of them in the media has become the main way for many to exist. And the new media allow them to participate at will, repeatedly and without limits so as to be ever present and not to be forgotten.

The new media, especially the television, the Internet, and the social media, have created a world in parallel to the real world, a virtual world where the most important thing is to speak about what one does or intends to do, or to get others to speak of it. This has become more important than actually doing it. One's image is more important than one's identity. What matters is not what one is truly, but what one passes for, one's appearance rather than oneself.

Presenting oneself thus through the media is a contrivance and an illusion. Sooner or later reality, which always has the last word, catches up. Self-satisfaction is replaced by dissatisfaction, dejection, and then depression.

A Relationship More Important Than an Identity

The hyper-communicative nature of the new media imperils the identity of the person and the person's consciousness of it. Permanently in communication in all directions, *homo connecticus* lives only in and through relationships, which for him become more important than his identity. It is true that the person needs relationship to exist, for his being is founded upon his relationships with God and with his parents. Then it develops through his relationships with his teachers, blossoming through relationships first with friends then with his spouse and his family. However, his identity is not defined by the relationship alone and cannot be reduced to it. Indeed, beyond a certain level, relationships can harm the identity so much as to destroy it.

The hyper-relational nature of the new media is to some extent dangerous for the personality. If it is too much with others, it has no time to be with itself. The person needs solitude as much as, if not more than, relationships to develop and blossom. This is borne out by the experience of hesychast spirituality, which grew up in the Christian East as the ultimate means of self-development. The term "hesychia" means calm, isolation, and solitude.

Psychiatrists are aware of many cases of emotional collapse, which are often marked by symptoms of depression, and are caused by self-forgetfulness in people who are totally immersed in social activities. They also know the importance of solitude for self-construction through facing up to oneself. This is what Pascal emphasized long ago when he said, "All the troubles of men come from one thing only, which is that they do not know how to dwell at rest in a room."[164]

The Ill Effects of Transparency

Another phenomenon linked to the development of the new media that imperils personal identity is the transparency that comes from their use. This transparency does not allow others to see a person as he really is. The person generally presents himself behind a mask or a caricature that he makes using the tricks made available by the media themselves. Moreover, he never appears in fullness and truth since the media edit what he expresses. They show only an aspect and image of the whole, creating a digital or virtual reality out of sounds images and written texts.

Self-exposure and transparency are not simply sought by individuals themselves but are encouraged by the media, especially the television. The audience of tele-reality programs is enhanced in this way through the voyeurism of a section of the public, its envy of those in the program and its desire to take their place, because of how the participants, by immodestly exposing their private lives, gain fame independent of their qualities, merits, or efforts. The reality of those who expose themselves in this way is further diminished and deformed by the staging of their show in advance that involves massive manipulation both before and after the act.

Although the exposure of the person by the media is diminished and modified by their wiles, even though it may be false, it is still a factor favoring transparency and externalization that eliminates inner life and thus attacks the person's very identity. This is so whether it is involuntary, voluntary, or actively sought.

Everything about one's private life becomes visible to all and sundry through smartphone conversations in public spaces, through blogs open to all and through photo albums posted online. As we have already seen, this destroys the natural boundary between public and private life and ends by damaging the person, for his inner balance requires much intimacy mixed in with some secrecy. Even in very close relationships, between those who are intimately linked, a certain mystery absolutely must be preserved. It is at the foundation of the person as a being who is unique, completely original and with mysterious depths that cannot be fathomed.

The transparency aroused or imposed by the new media, whether it is desired or not, is psychologically and spiritually destructive of the person. Many rush to their own destruction by going to extremes and ceaselessly recording everything they do, even at its most intimate, and posting it on the Internet.

The Externalization of the Person and the Impoverishment of Inner Life

Those who use the new media lose the initiative in their inner life and can no longer manage it. They are always on the watch for external stimuli, which they use for guidance. So, it is these stimuli that organize their lives and define the henceforth random path of their activities.

There is no space left for those times of solitude that contribute to the construction and stability of psychological and spiritual life. There are no more times for the silence that is required for deep thought and the contemplation that nourishes spiritual life. The flow of inner life is constantly interrupted by phone calls that distract the attention with their ring tones, by emails, or by tweets with their sonorous alerts. The habit of immediately reacting and replying further fragments inner life and turns the life of the soul into a chain of inarticulate events.

When no messages arrive, they are actively sought by sending text messages, tweets, or emails to get replies and to re-activate the chain of correspondence. *Homo connecticus* can no longer accept dead time, those periods of silence and withdrawal from the world that allow reflection or prayer. The need to fill up the time becomes an obsession that hides the truth: that it is this connected activity that in fact creates the void.

Connected man has become incapable of existing by himself and in relation to God. His only existence is social. He has got the idea that the only possible value of his existence is in the public domain. For him, to exist is to be able to be in contact at every moment, to be seen, heard, and localized all the time. It is to be present for others through the messages and photos that he sends. It is also to reveal and exhibit himself to others or before others.

He uses his telephone indiscreetly, speaking in his normal voice in public places to be overheard by all. He exposes himself in forums and blogs, discussing the most intimate details of his life. In all this he shows a complete loss of natural modesty and completely externalizes his inner life by publishing and exposing what is most intimate and personal. The boundary between public and private life is blurred so much that it disappears, leading to a form of de-personalization.

What seems at first to be a way to be freed from preoccupations, disquiet, and anxiety—a kind of therapy—is soon seen to be a source of new anxieties. Those who expose themselves thus not only empty out and impoverish themselves, but also expose themselves to the sometimes malevolent gaze of others, ready to judge, to mock, and to reject.

The life of the world is also impoverished. Permanent gossip on the phone, in forums, and blogs changes life itself into a commentary on life and parallels real existence with the virtual. Significant in this respect is the permanent need to take pictures of oneself and those close to one and of one's surroundings. It is as though the existence of photographic and digital records was more real and valuable than existence itself. Philippe Breton, in his book on *L'Utopie de la communication* remarks:

> *Homo communicans* is a being with no inner life who lives in society with no secrets. He is a being immersed in a social world who only exists through exchange of information in a society made transparent by the new "communication machines." These qualities of communicating

man, which have served to nourish modern man's ideals, can be seen as so many different paths to the human degradation produced by the torment of the twentieth century.[165]

The Increase of Emotion and Diminishing of Affection (Empathy, Compassion, etc.)

Certain analysts have found that the emotions of those who use the new media are enhanced, but their affections, especially their powers of empathy and compassion, are diminished. It is important to establish these distinctions. It is clear that the television acts powerfully on the emotions of those who watch it. Even the news, which is supposed to be the most objective of television programs, does this. It is supposed to view events from a distance, but in fact it emphasizes those facets of its subject that excite the emotions and exploits them to the hilt. This is often achieved with images, or with high-impact clips, which are especially good at arousing emotions. They can have such an impact that today's politicians often alter their decisions as a function of the emotions the media arouse in the population. Their lack of a critical vision often turns out to have catastrophic effects when, as is often the case, it can later be seen that the images were manipulated, staged, edited, or even fabricated. The Internet has similar effects, for the huge number of sites where the irresponsible can express their views encourages the spread of rumors, fake news, and photos or videos, which have been manipulated or taken out of context.

Looking at this from another viewpoint, one can see that the abstract nature of the media that enable communication and the way they mask the presence and reality of those in communication, by reducing it to the image, the voice, or the written word, greatly diminishes sentiments of affection in such relationships. We have already mentioned the dehumanizing aspects of text messages, emails, and tweets. Any form of polite introduction or conclusion is eliminated for brevity. So the sentiments of respect, friendship, affection, and social solidarity that lie behind their formality are lost.

Nicholas Carr considers that the new media, and especially the Internet, weaken good feelings toward those around us, especially the deeper and more subtle sentiments of empathy and compassion.[166] This is due to their speed, and the rapid reactions required of their users, and to the near endemic state of distraction that they provoke. This is backed up by a study conducted by a research group at the University of South Carolina, special-ized in the investigation of emotions. They show that normally, from his own experience of physical pain, a person is able to feel compassion imme-diately for another who suffers in the same way. But if he is engaged in rapid activity, he is unable to feel such emotions, since they need time to develop.[167] According to one of these researchers, even personal morality is compromised by most activities with the new media.[168]

The New Media as Elements of Regression

The new media can be clearly seen as contributing to regression in the sense of Freudian psychoanalysis. According to Freud, the psychology of a child develops through a certain number of stages. At each stage, the child feels a particular pleasure that must be abandoned in order to reach the next stage of development. If the child finds it hard to adapt to this new stage, then he may be brought to regress to the previous stage to find again the pleasures he once knew. This will serve as a reference point for him in his adult life to which he may return for a certain psychological comfort when he encounters difficulties that he cannot stand and cannot overcome. For Freudian psychoanalysis, addiction to tobacco, alcohol, drugs, or overeating is explained as manifestations of regression.

For many of our contemporaries, the various kinds of addiction to the new media are also manifestations of regression. The individual indulges in the lonely pleasures that they offer so as to flee from or to get round the various difficulties of the modern world with its multitude of frustra-tions. These are found in the workplace (unemployment, lack of security, stress, etc.) and in the relationships of life (loneliness, unstable marriages and friendships, difficulties with family members).

At a milder but still significant level, we have already alluded to the regression revealed by the need to feel at all times one's smartphone in one's pocket, or close to hand, just like a child's comforter. It is a reassuring object that can drive off the anxiety caused by a world felt as lonely or menacing.

A Field That Favors Narcissism

The Internet and Facebook have become fields where narcissism can easily develop and show itself using the cameras integrated into computers and smartphones. They make it easy to photograph and film oneself all the time and to publish the resulting videos and photos at once. Photographs of oneself (*selfies*) and their publication are major phenomena of modern society.

Not so long ago people had themselves photographed with others. They were less concerned with a representation of themselves than with the record of a meeting or a community. When photographed alone, it was against the background of a landscape as a record of a journey, a visit, or of beautiful countryside. Traditional photography required a certain distance between the camera and the subject and had to be done by another person. Here again, it implied a relationship.

A selfie is generally a photograph of one person only taken by the same person as a close up. This sets up the individual as the absolute center of importance, not for others, but for himself. The camera becomes a mirror through which the user sends himself his own image. Then he publishes it, seeking the appreciation of others in a way that reflects his pure love for himself. This is clearly narcissism, another form or regression according to Freud. Narcissism is an attitude found in a small child, referred to as the stage of the mirror. The psychologist Henri Wallon situates it at around the age of 9 months. The child will get beyond this stage as he learns to relate to others and to love them.

The narcissism developed by the new media shows itself in the different ways of exposing oneself, be they on Internet sites or in Facebook accounts. These are supposed to favor relationships, but in general simply allow one to boast. For this reason, *homo connecticus* embellishes the image he projects of himself in every possible way. He ends by constructing a virtual being that, not only for his friends but even for himself, parallels his reality and even replaces it. The new media reinforce the relevance of this thought of Pascal:

> We are not happy with the life we have within us and in our being: we wish to live in the idea which others have of an imaginary life; and for this we force ourselves to put on appearances. We constantly work to embellish and preserve this imaginary being whilst neglecting the true being.[169]

The social networks allow us to turn toward others, but not altruistically. If someone wants to know everything about other people, it is so that they may know everything about him: voyeurism at the service of narcissism. Like all other types of regression of which it is one, narcissism is a flight from a difficult or aggressive environment that one finds hard to bear. In his famous book, *The Culture of Narcissism*, Christopher Lasch wrote: Narcissism appears realistically to represent the best way of coping with the tensions and anxieties of modern life, and the prevailing social conditions therefore tend to bring out narcissistic traits that are present, in varying degrees, in everyone.[170]

Hypercommunication, Hyperstress, Hyperactivity: Hyperfatigue, Burn Out, and Depression

The new media allow permanent, immediate communication, free of cost. Coupled with the needs listed above of avoiding boredom and loneliness, existing in the media, as well as economic and social imperatives linked to work and the like, this has led to a digital world of hyper-communication, hyper-stress, and hyper-activity. The users of the new media have acquired a nervous fatigue on top of all their other activities. This is due to the following.

- Certain peculiarities of the new media; the sense of vision is over-stressed by attention to the screen and following the ceaseless flow of images; the hand is overstressed by rapid repetition of delicate movements; the mental and intellectual faculties become disjointed and unstructured through the continuous change and flow of content and, on the Internet, by prompts to open new links.

- Permanent external stress from telephone calls, multiplied by smartphones, from the alerts of mailboxes and social media, and the persistent inner temptation to consult the mailbox and the Facebook account and to follow links on the web.

Multitasking, implied by the presence and simultaneous alerts of several media at once, involves a great deal of task changing at the expense of the nervous system. As Maggie Jackson remarks, " ... the brain takes time to change goals, remember the rules needed for the new task, and block out cognitive interference from the previous, still-vivid activity"[171]; but even navigating the Internet poses the same kind of problem. As Nicholas Carr remarks, "On the Net, where we routinely juggle not just two but several mental tasks, the switching costs are all the higher."[172]

The tiredness built up during the day and especially, more intensely, in the evening causes sleep problems, so tiredness is increased and not assuaged. It has been observed that sleep problems have greatly increased in the population in recent decades. Many treatments have been developed as remedies, but with only small success, for the cause of the problem persists, often unidentified. In fact it is the psychological disorder and fatigue, produced by the new media, which are the cause. Often, it is enough to stop using them altogether for several days for sweet sleep to return.

Accumulated nervous fatigue leads to decompensations, which can end in depression,[173] but more often take the form of burn out. This disorder, which is beginning to be recognized as a work-related sickness, is certainly due in part to professional hyperactivity. Commerce puts pressure on its employees so as to increase their productivity and profitability. But over and above the extra accumulated tiredness produced by using the new media at work, the nervous system is also affected by the same activities outside work.

As we have already pointed out in a previous chapter, the new media, especially the portable phone and emails, have removed for many the boundary between work and leisure that once was theirs, between the professional and social sphere and the private sphere of the family. Employees can be contacted at any time and are given tasks to perform even when at home or on holiday during the time that used to be called "free" but is no more.

In addition to the tiredness caused by the use of the new media imposed by employers both at work and elsewhere, there is the tiredness caused by the use of these media during leisure. Television, video games, the Internet, and social media are examples. This is made worse, especially when linked to addiction or dependency, if they lead the user to give up some of his hours of rest or sleep, especially at night.

Addictive Effects

Among the worst problems caused by the new media are addictions and dependencies. In extreme cases, which are in fact quite common, the new media act as a drug: many people today are driven to use them in the same way as others are driven to use traditional narcotics and are dependent in the same way.

It is known that almost all drug users who are well-off use them to escape from an inner or outer life which they find difficult. The drugs act immediately on the brain and the psychological faculties to dull the consciousness or to plunge the user into an imaginary world. Many psychiatrists and psychoanalysts have observed with the same conviction that "screens are used today mostly to try to forget the difficulties and suffering of daily life."[174]

This purpose in the use of screens is already present in infancy as research at the London School of Economics has shown:

> Psychological approaches suggest that people use the internet excessively to compensate for social or psychological difficulties, and deficits in personal wellbeing in terms of their everyday offline life. Studies have linked sensation-seeking (a tendency to pursue excitement and sensory pleasure), loneliness and emotional problems (such as depression and low self-confidence) to excessive internet use (Mehroof & Griffiths, 2010). According to this theory, children who are psychologically vulnerable are more likely to be at risk of excessive internet use since they are trying to compensate for a problem in their offline lives. One major qualification here is that there is little agreement about whether these psychological characteristics are a result, or a cause, of excessive internet use, as illustrated by the earlier anecdote of Martin. We can expect that where a child already experiences social and psychological difficulties, this increases the risk of that child becoming involved in excessive internet use. It is also worth noting, as with Martin, that the child may not see their internet use as a problem but as a positive, coping response to other social, emotional and psychological challenges in the child's life. On the other hand, emotional and psychological problems can increase when a child experiences excessive internet use.[175]

When speaking of addiction, "cyber-addiction" must be distinguished from "cyber-assisted addiction." Cyber-addiction is an addiction to certain means of communication, especially the Internet and social media. Those who suffer from cyber-assisted addiction are not addicted to the new media themselves, but to the realities to which they give quick, easy, and unlimited access: online games, sex, compulsive purchases, etc. The new media are just as responsible for these latter addictions. They provide permanent encouragement for them, and the means and tools to put them into effect. By their very nature, they are deeply involved in addictions. The addicts are generally seen, as the words of those near to them show, as dependent on their television, their game console, their smartphone, or their computer.

The content seems to matter little. It can be changed at will to fill some passing need created in the addict's mind.

Cyber-addictions and cyber-assisted addictions are linked through the Internet, since addiction to the Internet often opens the door to a cyber-assisted addiction. As the psychiatrists, Michel Hautefeuille and Dan Véléa have remarked: "it is the dream tool for someone drawn to addiction: it can provide whatever attracts the addict."[176]

The worst kinds of addiction are exclusive. They cause other tasks and relationships, which make up social life, to be abandoned for much of the day. Overall, an addiction can be defined in the same way as a passion in its traditional sense. Michel Hautefeuille and Dan Véléa have observed that the use becomes pathological "from the moment when behavior becomes exclusive, leading to collateral damage: long term abandonment of other centers of interest, the family, education and work. The addict lives only for the object of his addiction, excluding all else. His whole life and energy are concentrated on his obsession. Everything else becomes completely secondary and is gradually abandoned."[177]

The worst kinds of addiction to the new media should not blind us to its milder forms that still have negative effects on psychological life. Nowadays, many users of the new media are addicts without realizing it. They tend to see their dependency as unimportant compared to the worst addictions, and through use and habit have trivialized their behavior on the media by absorbing it into their general behavior in life.

Addiction in all its forms is marked by dependency of different degrees. It consists of a more or less irresistible attraction that indicates a more or less pressing need whose satisfaction brings a more or less conscious pleasure. If left unsatisfied it brings frustration, a feeling of missing out that gives rise to a more or less intense feeling of mental suffering. Apart from these inner gauges, the strength of addiction can be measured by the degree to which it degrades adaption to society and presence therein, first in the family, then in school or work, and finally in relations in general.

Psychologists have developed tests for measuring the degree of dependency. The best known is Orman's test, which applies to Internet use:

1. Do you spend more time than you think you should surfing the Net?
2. Do you feel you have a problem limiting the time you spend on the Net?

3. Have any of your friends or family members complained about the time you spend at your computer?
4. Do you find it hard to stay away from the Net for several days at a time?
5. Has either your work output or your personal relationships suffered as a result of spending too much time on the Net?
6. Are there particular areas of the Net, or types of files, you find hard to resist?
7. Do you have troubling controlling your impulses to purchase items, products, or services on the Net?
8. Have you tried, unsuccessfully, to curtail your use of the Net?
9. Do you derive much of your pleasure and satisfaction in life from being on the Net?
10. Up to three positive replies indicate a slight tendency to become addicted to the Internet.
11. Between four and six positive replies indicate a certain propensity to become addicted.
12. Between seven and nine positive replies indicates a strong tendency to addiction.

Although this test is designed to be used by psychologists who need a scale, it can be used by anyone to assess the nature of their own behavior.

A Space of Illusory Freedom

Because they give everyone the power to communicate immediately and permanently with the whole world, the new media seem to remove two major constraints on our freedom: space and time. They seem to offer our freedom a boundless field of action and the possibility of infinite choice between all the objects in the world to which they grant access.

However, as we have seen in the preceding chapters, the new media place a real restraint on personal freedom at several levels: political, through the surveillance and propaganda that they enable; economic, through the surveillance and exploitation of workers that they permit; and social through the abolition of the boundary between public and private life that they bring about.

Addiction to the new media, be it cyber-dependence or cyber-assisted dependence is another restriction on freedom in addition to the above. It is worse, since it restricts inner freedom, not simply outer freedom. It gives rise to the same kind of bondage as the passions, both in the modern psychological sense and in the spiritual sense. For these diminish the conscience and the will of the person. They subject the person to the strong attraction of external factors that appear seductive, but in reality are insubstantial, imaginary in the case of the classic passions and virtual for those that attract to the new media. They also act on him through external mechanisms that marshal his energy and disperse his powers in a stream without substance or consistency. As Philippe Breton has observed, while man traditionally seemed to be directed from within by himself, the new man is firstly a communicator, his interior open to the world. The messages he receives do not arise within him "but rather from his environment. He does not act. He reacts, and not to an action. He reacts to a reaction."[178]

This confirms what we have already observed: the Net can be seen as a spider's web, or as a fishing net, which imprisons all those who plunge into it; and the networks as cords or chains that bind and hold captive their users. Ordinary social life allows us to see how more and more people are ever more strongly bound to their smartphones, to another world whose echo reaches them through their absently worn earphones with wires resembling leashes whose pull they follow.

CHAPTER 11

≋

Dumbing Down the Mind

For the wisdom of their wise men shall perish, and the understanding
of their prudent men shall be hidden.

—Isaiah 29:14 (NKJV)

God only knows what it's doing to our children's brains.

—Sean Parker, former president of Facebook

It is becoming more and more obvious that the use of the new media affects
the user's mental processes and dumbs them down. These effects are
most marked in childhood. From their earliest age, children are subjected
to all the new media, especially the television and video games, and it shows
in their school results at various stages of their education. Adults are also
affected. Even when they have only recently begun to use the new media,
the negative effects on their mental processes soon show.

Short- and Long-Term Deterioration in School Results

Most studies agree that using the new media brings about a deterioration
in school results both short and long term.[179] This is explained by several
factors. First of all, the new media eat up time. Taken together, according
to a recent study,[180] they reduce by between 28% and 36% the time devoted
to lessons and homework. They also increase tiredness by burning up the

user's energy and by reducing the time and quality of sleep. This has an impact on wakefulness, attention, and memory, and on mental development in general. The third factor is the way they reduce the user's attentiveness and concentration so much that more and more children and adolescents find it hard to attend for more than a few minutes to a talk or a written text.

They also have other effects. They reduce linguistic competence through changes in the way language is used and by a reduction in the vocabulary employed. The constant flow of information that they provide removes the stimulus of reflection and leaves little time for reading, which is so important for learning. Worse, the users are cut off from those who provide their education, their parents and teachers. Indeed, a typical primary school pupil spends per year more time in front of a screen than with his teachers and parents combined. The interaction of children with their parents is essential for the psychological and intellectual development of the young. Its reduction greatly impedes the acquisition of language and the cognitive development linked to it.

Michel Desmurget refers to this when writing of the negative effects of the television:

> The television set will always lack one of the fundamental qualities of a teacher: interactivity. [...] The television does not nod approval to encourage a child's activity. It does not alter its words when it sees that they produce a blank expression on the child's face. It does not name the objects the child sees. It does not imitate the words which he pronounces. It does not correct the opinions he expresses. It does not reply to the sounds he makes. In the end, all these defects make the television a wretchedly pathetic teacher, and worse, a powerful destroyer of language. In this regard, the television does not merely pour out its vile incompetence passively over our children. It also works at a deeper lever to mutilate sociability in the family. When the television is on, even in the background, the child hears fewer words and speaks less, in shorter phrases, taking part in fewer two way conversations. In other words, with fewer words at the earlier stages of his development, the child grows up less at ease with words and with less intelligence.[181]

In general the new media, which are themselves projectors of activity, reduce children to a state of passivity and mental lethargy. This contrasts with the intense activity of the little fingers on the remote control of the television, the game console, the keyboard, the mouse, or the touchscreen. They encourage the enjoyment of facile audiovisual entertainment at the expense of the discipline, sense of effort, patience, perseverance, and sacrifice, which are required for the serious learning of any skill whatever. This passivity and lethargy in front of the screen leads to impulsiveness and wild, disorderly hyperactivity when they are removed, as in the normal setting of the home, or in the classroom. Many parents and teachers complain bitterly about how deeply they disturb family life and school in general.

The negative effects of the new media on school results are felt short term and also long term. Some recent research has shown how the more a child watches television before the age of 3, the less he attends to his school work at the age of 10. Participation, effort, and curiosity are all diminished. Some other research has shown how each hour spent in front of the television between the ages of 5 and 11 increases by 50% the probability of attention deficit at the age of 13. Yet more research shows that each hour spent in front of the television at 14 years of age increases the probability of attention deficit at 16 by 44%. There is a whole body of research conducted over the last 40 years that shows how rapid audiovisual effects play a massive role in producing attention deficits in children and adolescents.[182] When attention is reduced, the whole mental apparatus is affected.[183] Several studies have shown that there is a negative correlation between the amount of television watched and the probability of obtaining a university degree.[184]

Comprehensive Dumbing Down

The negative effects of the new media on children's mental processes are sure to carry through to their adult life. Not only are certain habits acquired, often irreversibly, but also certain neural processes become hard-wired into the brain. And even the mental processes of adults who have not been deformed by the new media in their childhood can be damaged once they start using the new media too much, which often happens.

In his famous work *The Shallows*, Nicholas Carr shows how using the new media, and especially the Internet is shown to have negative effects on everyone. It not only affects their thought process itself, but also what this thought presupposes: use of language and the related matters of attention and concentration. It affects language quality both externally (the style) and internally (the continuity, rigor, and coherence). These negative effects are due to different factors and are seen in various ways.

The Image Is More Important Than the Text

We have seen in an earlier chapter how the image has taken more and more space in the media, crowding out the words. The more the media use images, the more they replace conceptual thought, founded on language with what linguists call "iconic thought." This is a rudimentary pre-linguistic thought form that small children use before they learn to speak and that adults use when asleep. It can also be found to a lesser degree in certain of the more developed animals.

This elementary kind of thought depends on feelings and imagination and very little on logical reflection, especially when the images flow fast and free. The television, especially, has become a machine for pouring forth images and only rarely, on cultural channels and in cultural documentaries transmitted late at night, does it give real food for thought. The recent launch of an animal channel takes this trend to the limit, where the media provide images without the slightest place for human thought.

Giovanni Sartori considers our day, dominated by the image, to be the post-thought era (*post-pensiero*), a new age that follows on from the age of thought and that brings forth a new kind of man, *home videns* who replaces *homo sapiens.* He shows how the television in particular "creates images and erases concepts. It makes our powers of abstraction fade away, and with them, our ability to understand."[185] In other words, the entire intellectual realm is gravely sick with an illness that affects the whole world.

Shrinking Language (Vocabulary and Grammar)

The Poverty of Language on the Television

Pride of place given to the image undoubtedly helps to dumb down the language used on the television, which in turn dumbs down the language of those who watch it. George Steiner has said that "we are witnessing a progressive demolition of language which is being drowned by the image, especially through the internet."[186]

Even what remains of the language is qualitatively degraded. The aim of the big television companies is to gain the largest possible audience so as to maximize advertising revenue. To this end, they descend to the lowest common denominator of culture. They aim for programs that will be popular and easy for the spectators to view, sparing them any intellectual effort, which might drive them away. They also aim for the lowest common linguistic denominator, using language that is easily understood by the greatest possible audience. Normal French language, excluding scientific and technical vocabulary, contains between 60,000 and 75,000 words.[187] Retained vocabulary (potentially usable and clearly understandable) is around 30,000 words for a cultivated person, and between 2,500 and 6,000 words for a high school student. In daily life, an adult typically uses around 3,000, and a high school student between 800 and 1,600. However, most things can be expressed with just 600 words, which are the most commonly used and make up 90% of every written text.[188]

These 600 words make up the basic vocabulary of the television. Those who speak, presenters, journalists, and guests, are encouraged to restrict themselves to this. If they are more adventurous, they are either cut off, or a commentary is added to explain what is being said. Journalists often do this when guests stray beyond the limits as can often happen in live interviews.

The poverty of the television's language helps to impoverish the vocabulary of those who watch it for several hours every day. Its impact on the school results of the young is obvious. Combined with other factors linked to the television, it has been assessed as negative in pedagogical studies.[189] This linguistic deficit is also found in adults who spend several hours per day in front of the television, very few of whom choose to watch cultural programs.

The Programmed Degradation of Style in the Media

It is not just television entertainment where the language is dumbed down. The same occurs with journalistic language in all the media. It has become a standardized language where every form of expression except the simplest is eliminated. There are no long sentences with complex syntax and a rich vocabulary. Politicians and senior administrators trained in France's leading schools, Science-Po and the ENA, are judged on their ability as orators. Their grades reflect the brilliance of their speeches. But when they move on to their first jobs they are required to learn a dumbed down form of French. For instance, a recent article in the press revealed that a minister had followed a program to train him to speak in public using a vocabulary limited to 500 words.

Even the more serious newspapers with educated readers are tempted to simplify their language as much as possible. This inevitably means that the thoughts expressed lose their depth and subtlety and their ability to convince, for these are closely linked to the richness of language and even to its complexity. Journalists are not satisfied by dumbing down their own language. They also try to dumb down what those whom they interview have to say. Philippe Breton remarks:

A specialist or an expert is not allowed to speak if the language used is not purged of anything which might be thought dull or hard to understand. It is better to show his picture and to accompany it with a text composed and read out by a journalist. The comments of an expert should be an entertainment for the public who should have a good time and above all, never have their ignorance revealed. The presentation must always give the impression of certainty, of covering everything, whereas the development of knowledge requires the identification and acceptance of areas of ignorance. [...] From this all kinds of manipulation are possible when the knowledge is translated into sound bites. The most common is to rewrite the interview [...]. This tendency has recently become so marked that some experts wonder if they will continue to give interviews when they know how their text may be re-written several times before it is broadcast and will probably be emptied of much of its substance. The strong protests which this systematic practice arouses are met with the reply that it matters little what one says of a subject provided one speaks of it. The main thing is to be in the media so as to exist, to be at the "center," even if the message is, in the end, of minor importance. Of course, the text of an interview is not always understood by the journalist for in all professions there are the skilled and less skilled. Even if it is, what usually disappears from the text is the thread of the argument. Building up knowledge or defending an idea is usually done through a process of developing arguments, which is why a certain concentration is needed to follow it. A moderator will take a sentence here and a sentence there, not necessarily in the same order. He will use the text as though it consisted of a string of detachable sound bites. News works fine with discontinuity but building knowledge is a continuous process. The author often finds that he cannot recognize the results as what he said. The only way this can be avoided is to try to encapsulate an important point of one's reasoning in a sound bite. Politicians know that the best argued and most closely reasoned of speeches will almost never be reported with its logic intact. So they have become adept at producing striking sound bites based on rhetorical figures or shock phrases. The problem is that these stylistic devices are ill adapted to the development of a rigorously reasoned argument.[190]

The Negative Effects of the Text Message

The degradation of language is even more obvious in the new ways of communication enabled by computer, tablets, and smartphones. Text messages have come to occupy an important place in communication for they cost little and their brevity allows them to be composed with little effort. This brevity is linked to a desire for rapidity, which is often unnecessary. The message is often sent on impulse and compulsively read. This leads to the use of phonetic abbreviations that are far from the original spelling, and to linguistic constructions that are marginal or deformed compared to the reference language.[191] All this is accompanied by a neglect of grammar and spelling with the content taking complete precedence over the form. Entire sentences may be reduced to a string of the initial letters of the words they contain,[192] or to sounds more or less well rendered.[193]

Clearly one might see this as a system of abbreviations like those once used for telegraphs and telegrams, or as a form of shorthand. One may also see it as a "newtongue" with its own linguistic structure, remaining related, since it is more or less articulated, to humanity's other languages or dialects. Nevertheless, its daily use in coexistence or symbiosis with normal language, rather than in a specific setting, has negative effects with respect to the official reference language.

This kind of dumbed down language is very widely used by the young and even infants. It has a very negative effect on their linguistic training and their mastery of language. It gives them the impression that respect for the dictionary of the language (vocabulary) and its grammar (syntax and spelling) is not needed for communication. It demotivates them and may leave them indifferent to their lessons. This will not fail to have an impact on how well they master different disciplines in school that all require at every level, even in mathematics, a mastery of their language. Their understanding of lessons and their homework are compromised, either leaving them as academic failures or greatly reducing their performance. They are also handicapped in their social or professional lives when they need to understand instructions and compose documents correctly.

Using the language of text messages does not directly degrade the reference language. There is little contamination and no effect on the spoken language since it is essentially a method of transcription that gives precedence to phonetics. It is the way it is used by certain sections of society that is degraded, creating different linguistic, intellectual, and cultural levels, which enhance social inequality.

Shrinking Language and Thought with Short Messages

Tweets and emails usually have a higher linguistic level than text messages. Tweets are published to the world and may be read by people from different levels of society, which makes their writers more careful of their composition. Emails have largely replaced letters and although a degraded language may be used, they have still preserved certain forms of the traditional letter. But along with the text message, both are part of the trend to brevity.

Unfortunately, this brevity that is becoming dominant in communication tends strongly to undermine thought. It is true that there are short forms of expression, which may sometimes be found in tweets, which are the quintessence of thought, such as proverbs, sayings, apothegms, and especially the haïkus of Japanese poetry. These convey the experience and wisdom of the ages, or universal truths, sometimes in exquisitely worked verse to encode the meaning. How different they are from those phrases quickly composed on the keyboard and shot out without thought or reflection to convey a crude impression, or the feeling of the moment.

George Steiner considers that it is not simply the multitude of images that undermines our language but also the abbreviated forms of expression used in the new media. "Language is devoured by the obsessive minimalism of electronic codes such as the ever more compressed messages emitted by mobile phones."[194]

The Negative Impact on Reading

The negative impact of the new media on reading is the most commonly quoted problem related to their effects on cultural impoverishment and dumbing down the mind. This is seen in several ways.

Connected Man Reads Little

The hours spent watching television have been time taken away from reading for certain people of all ages. The computer and the Internet have stolen yet more hours from reading and so has the smartphone. There are several factors that explain why connected man hardly reads at all. In general, the mono-media of books is confronted with screens everywhere, which project easily accessible audiovisual material through a rich selection of multimedia devices; and this has caused the culture of the written word to ebb in our societies. Basically, the consumption of free time by the new media downgrades reading.[195] Permanent connection to different media all at once produces continuous distraction that is hardly favorable for allowing the time, attention, and concentration required by reading.

Because of the factors mentioned above, reading requires an effort that modern man is less and less able to furnish. The reader is always active, while a user of the new media is generally passive, taking the easy way. Faced with such easy and attractive entertainments, children and adolescents, first and foremost, make little effort and hardly read at all.[196] This clearly has a negative effect on their reading and writing skills,[197] and their general cultural level. Later, when they grow up it will affect their reading as adults, for it has been clearly shown that it is during one's early years that the taste and habit of reading are acquired.

Another reason is related to the Internet and the computer in general. Many published books both in their official and pirated versions are available in digital form. They can be cheaply or freely acquired and downloaded in a few seconds. Many students and even university professors frantically download quantities of publications. They are like compulsive collectors of objects. Their main motive is the desire to possess everything and not to miss anything, quite independently of any actual use they may make of them.

Books and articles saved on hard drives are not the same as books placed on the shelves, which always remind us of their existence. Instead, they are soon forgotten in a virtual morass. What is worse is that saving a book onto one's hard drive gives the false impression that it has been read, as though the memory of the computer was magically linked with one's own.

Connected Man Reads Badly

Besides images, videos, and sounds, the Internet proposes an enormous quantity of written matter. It takes little effort to find it. It proposes or imposes itself uninvited. There are many programs, plug-ins, or applications available on computers, with fonts of every size and color, which access these textual resources as desired. Moreover, multi-purpose tablets are available that allow newspapers, magazines, and books to be read in comfort. Among such devices, well suited to reading, are the iPad from Apple and the Kindle from Amazon. Almost all newspaper publishers now offer digital editions in parallel with, and cheaper than, their printed editions. They can be read on these devices, some of which have a display that closely resembles the page of a book. These tablets and readers are very practical: slim and light, their memories can store a great number of books and magazines and avoid the difficulties of weight and volume when traveling.

Digital books are cheaper than printed books, and the classics can be downloaded free of charge. So, objectively, the new media offer as many or even more texts as were available in the past, and allow them to be read with ease.

Despite all this, connected man reads little and reads badly. The main reason for this is that the new media, especially the Internet, have, in practice, changed the way we approach these texts. On-screen, a text is shown as images. This fact is not altered by the excellent definition of the pages shown by good-quality readers, which resemble closely the pages of a printed book. The images simply have higher resolution.

When these texts, presented as images, are read on-screen, with the pages following each other in a flow of images, our visual senses are stimulated. These have already been overdeveloped in modern man by the television and other audiovisual media. And as Giovanni Sartori has shown, they have changed *homo sapiens* into *homo videns*.[198] For this reason, an on-screen text is scanned like an image, rather than carefully read. Normally only a few lines are taken in.

Jacob Nielsen filmed the movements of the eyes of 232 people reading on the web. He found that the vast majority did not read the text line by line as with a book, but they jumped quickly from the top to the bottom of the page in a movement that traced out the form of the letter "F." They read the first few lines, then jumped further down the page to read the left-hand part of a few more, then scanned the rest of the left-hand side of the page.[199] The same author conducted a second study using a database constructed by German researchers. They analyzed the way twenty-five people used their computers over 100 days, on average, to determine how long they took to read 59,573 web pages.[200] Nielsen found that if there are more words on a page, more time is spent on reading it, but not much more. The user spent only 4.4 seconds extra for an extra 100 words. Since a good reader can read about 18 words in 4.4 seconds, Nielsen concluded that the average reader of the web reads at best only about 20% of its text.[201]

Traditionally, reading was done slowly. The reader took his time. In contrast, reading on the screen is done quickly at a speed imposed by the rhythm of the media, or encouraged by the ambiance of rapidity and reactivity that is theirs, and by the physical and mental frenzy with which they are most often used.

The German research referred to by Nielsen found that most web pages are looked at for a maximum of 10 seconds. Less than one page out of ten is looked at for more than 2 minutes. Their results back up one of the main conclusions of Nielsen's first study concerning reading in the normal sense of the word: "Clearly people don't read the pages they visit even for a second!"

Websites are programmed to measure the time passed by each visitor on each page, but are rather ashamed to admit the results that are not in their favor. ClickTale, which provides the software to analyze how the commercial web pages are read, analyzed all the data collected in May and June 2008 of the behavior of a million visitors to the sites of their clients in various countries. They found that in most countries people spend on average between 19 and 27 seconds on a page including the time to load it (1.1 to 5.5 seconds).[202]

What is paradoxical is that in spite of reading less and more quickly on each page, the readers of digital texts spend more time on the process of reading than those who read a text of the same length in printed form. The reason is that readers of digital texts tend to stray onto other pages to which the links draw them, or search for parallel material with their search engine while trying to read the text.[203]

The reader of a text on the screen does not generally pause to take in words or expressions unless they are key words about the subject, which he had in mind before starting, or hypertext links, which he uses to stray from the subject. He does not revisit earlier phrases or reflect as he reads. This is superficial reading with almost no effort to understand or to memorize. Each page leads on to the next and is straightway forgotten.

Of course rapid reading (diagonally) is not unique to digital texts. It is often used with printed texts, especially newspapers. But it was used to select articles of interest, which could then be read attentively from beginning to end. In some ways, as Nicholas Carr has said, it is just as important to be able to read diagonally as in depth. But it is different, and worrying, when skimming the surface has become our main method of reading. What once was done with the purpose of selecting what was worth reading in depth has now become an end in itself. It is our preferred way of collecting and understanding all sorts of information.[204]

Strange though it may seem, the physical reality of a book gives weight and reality to what is read, while the dematerialized book, read on a digital reader or on-screen as text, makes the book seem insignificant. It makes the text lose some of its reality and density, leaving it light and inconsequential. Many traditional readers have said how the physical existence of a book, which can be seen in its entirety, felt, and touched, has an important role in the relationship both to the book and to the text, affecting the way it is read.

One of the features of digital text on the Internet is that it is loaded with hypertext links. From key words or expressions, these direct the reader to other pages where can be found, as in footnotes, explanations, or extra information. However, these hypertext links are very different from footnotes, printed in small font to show that they depend on and are secondary to the main text. They can be quickly examined and we may choose whether or not to read them so as not to stray too much from the main text. Hypertext links seem to be optional but are actually a permanent temptation to the reader. He does not know what lies behind them and is drawn to click on them lest he misses something important. He is driven by idle curiosity or a need for distraction. These links are designed to capture our attention and so disperse it. They constantly break the reader's concentration and also contribute to making reading on the screen less serious, more superficial, and overall less profitable than reading a printed text.

Reading on the screen brings into play other forms of dispersion. One of them is that such reading almost always incites the reader to use the search engine to find out more about the facts or people evoked. Another temptation to dispersion is that both on a computer and on the Internet the reader has a multitude of sources at his disposal and is tempted to flit from one to another without stopping to look at any of them properly.

Digital reading is marked with the same frenzy and instability as is every other activity on the new media. The jerky rhythm of the reader's brief scans of short extracts from each source ends by molding his thought itself, which comes to require the same jerky rhythm when it takes its material from the web.

Another source of distraction to reading is the flow of emails and text messages that are received by the same device used for reading: computer, tablet, or smartphone. These may be heralded by a signal that has become for almost every connected man a call to instant consultation.

Digital reading is accompanied by a reduction in attention that is also due to the mental fatigue resulting from digital hyperactivity and the continual disturbance experienced in this environment. Nicholas Carr writes of this:

.... the extensive activity in the brains of surfers also points to why deep reading and other acts of sustained concentration become so difficult online. The need to evaluate links and make related navigational choices, while also processing a multiplicity of fleeting sensory stimuli, requires constant mental coordination and decision making, distracting the brain from the work of interpreting text or other information. Whenever we, as readers, come upon a link, we have to pause, for at least a split second, to allow our prefrontal cortex to evaluate whether or not we should click on it. The redirection of our mental resources, from reading words to making judgments, may be imperceptible to us—our brains are quick—but it's been shown to impede comprehension and retention, particularly when it's repeated frequently. As the executive functions of the prefrontal cortex kick in, our brains become not only exercised but overtaxed. In a very real way, the Web returns us to the time of *scriptura continua*, when reading was a cognitively strenuous act.[205]

Traditionally, reading took place in a quiet, relatively isolated setting for a relatively long period. However reading on the screen takes place for a short time in the noise and swarm of digital temptations and enticements. Each hypertext link and each claim on the attention is like an event that disturbs one's vacation.

Many bloggers on the Internet have realized that their readers are impatient and incapable of concentrating on a long text. They cannot read for long and have a phobia of any text too long to be seen at a glance in its entirety. So, the bloggers shorten their texts to a dozen or two lines, or even replace them with a string of short sentences. To keep the reader's attention and to provide him with all the distractions to which he is accustomed, they insert many hyperlinks, images, and videos. To survive, every text must become multimedia and multi-dimensional. It must bear within itself the paths that encourage us to abandon it. Through the multimedia, our relationship to the text becomes less stable, lighter, weaker, and fleeting.

Weakening of Reflection

Using the new media weakens our ability to reflect, both quantitatively and qualitatively. Reflection is not simply thought, a flow of descriptions, images, and ideas. It is an ordered process that involves the intuition backed by reason, with its logical categories and its rules of organization and argument, and by a critical spirit. As its name reveals, reflection is not a raw thought, but a way of examining it, developing it, and proving it. It means stepping back to a certain distance, and taking time.

The new media work almost without a pause, pouring forth a continuous flow of information that does not allow our thought to pause and examine itself. Our mental powers go with the flow, almost wholly reduced to dependence and passivity. The new media change time into a succession of instants, which prevents reflection, since to function reflection needs a relatively long time.

Urgency is the hallmark of the new media. Messages must be sent quickly. A rapid reply must be made to the phone or to emails. Texts and tweets must be sent at once to reply to requests or react to events. This speed prevents reflection, which generally needs time, except in the exceptionally rare case of real urgency.

Nicholas Carr has shown how using the Internet diverts our mental resources by forcing our brain to evaluate links and make decisions about navigation while handling a flow of fleeting stimuli to the senses. This permanent mental coordination for decision-making prevents the brain from seeking to understand what it reads, and even more, to reflect on it deeply.[206] Our era seems to justify the fear expressed by Heidegger in the middle of the last century: that technical progress would drown what is the very essence of our humanity, "meditative thought."[207] Information is only useful and enriching if it can be mastered by the intelligence that makes sense of it. But as Jean Baudrillard observes, "We live in a world with more and more information and less and less sense.[208]

Information Without Learning or Knowledge

Looking at their effects in the domain of culture and education we have seen how the new media, especially the Internet and the television, pour forth a flood of information. But it is hard to digest such a mass of information. It makes one's head spin and ends by destroying itself, for "too much information kills information."[209]

Even if the information can be digested, it still does not make for knowledge, which is not simply an accumulation of information. The nature of the new media means that information is generally received in scraps discontinuously and passively. It is not examined or put in order to be thoughtfully assimilated. Even when the information may be of high quality it can be seen that the users of the Internet "generally fail to ask the right questions or to sort the results or to rank their sources."[210] They also have difficulty in synthesizing whatever information they may have collected.

The sum of the information one receives cannot give knowledge in the true sense of the word, for knowledge rests on firm foundations. It formalizes information to give it unity and ranks it according to its importance and value within culture.[211] Information alone is not knowledge, which implies an in-depth understanding of its subject that has become, through reflection, one's personal possession.

Losing One's Memory

Another striking effect of the new media is how they make you lose your memory. Computers have the capacity to store huge quantities of information, and even more on associated storage devices such as external hard drives, USB keys, and DVDs, not to mention the "Cloud" on the servers of the service providers. This and the possibility of finding instantly any fact on the Internet give *homo connecticus* the impression that there is no need to make the personal effort to memorize these things.

These new inventions seem to have the advantage of sparing one the effort of memorizing anything or the need to recall and preserve the memory. They also are more reliable than the memory of man, which may not always register things perfectly and which may lose or modify what it recalls as time goes by, reconstructing them with gaps and distortions. We can see here an image of the famous reflections of Plato on writing in Phaedrus where King Thamus refuses the writing that the god Theuth has just invented, saying that it would give those who learn it an illusion of memory and knowledge.

> "O King," said Theuth, "This will make the Egyptians wiser and give them better memories; it is a specific both for the memory and for the wit." Thamus replied: "O most ingenious Theuth, the parent or inventor of an art is not always the best judge of the utility or inutility of his own inventions to the users of them. And in this instance, you who are the father of letters, from a paternal love of your own children have been led to attribute to them a quality which they cannot have; for this discovery of yours will create forgetfulness in the learners' souls, because they will not use their memories; they will trust to the external written characters and not remember of themselves. The specific which you have discovered is an aid not to memory, but to reminiscence, and you give your disciples not truth, but only the semblance of truth; they will be hearers of many things and will have learned nothing; they will appear to be omniscient and will generally know nothing; they will be tiresome company, having the show of wisdom without the reality."[212]

As Peter Sudermann has said, computers have changed memory into a mere index, and intelligence into the simple capacity of using this index. In fact, it leaves the memory empty of any significant content. It has the same relationship to true information as the telephone directory has to the people it lists, or the card index of a library to the books it contains. "Rather than memorize information, we now store it digitally and just remember what we stored." "Now the web teaches us to think like it does—as a tool for recall and connection." Unlike the hero of Ray Bradbury's novel, *Farenheit 451*, who memorized complete books, "We won't become books, we'll become their indexes and reference guides... preferring instead to know what's known, by ourselves and others, and where that knowledge is stored." So that in the end we have "rather little deep knowledge" left in our heads."[213]

Because this external store of information exists we refer to it every time we need something stored on the web, and so we no longer use our own faculty of memory and recall. We use the documents we have stored on our computer, or those from our near-permanent connection to the Internet, and it is no longer so effective to use our brain to store information. Why memorize the entire contents of a book when you could be using your brain to remember a quick guide to the library? Instead of remembering information we now store it in digital form and at best we remember only what we have stored,[214] for the frenzy of downloading may become so intense that it is not even possible to recall the titles of what was saved.

Weakening of the memory is not simply linked to the storage capacity of the new media, but also to the various ways in which digital culture eases some of the tasks of daily life. For example, with the phone numbers of all our contacts stored on our smartphone we no longer remember the phone numbers of those close to us. With calculators integrated into every smartphone we often become incapable of the simplest operations of arithmetic, let alone the more complex such as long division or the extraction of square roots that once could be done by anyone who had finished primary school.

The possibility of external memory does not merely externalize the memory but devalues it as well. Memorizing something personally seems like a waste of time and the effort of recall a useless waste of energy. This leaves a chasm between our modern digital civilization and the societies of old who valued memory so much that some of them deified it, like the ancient Greeks with their goddess Mnemosyne. Others likened it to a place where God is present and thought it to be a path to Him.[215] Memorizing great literary texts or sacred writings, even when copied or printed, was one of the basic tasks in school for young children.

The capacity for memory is very flexible. It develops when it is used and withers away when it is neglected. If rote learning was once one of the basic subjects in primary education, it was not primarily to introduce the young to the realm of literary culture, poetry, theatre, and the like, but because it trained the memory and improved it for every other subject studied. It is not some special gift, but intense and regular exercise of the memory that enables actors to learn in a few weeks their role in a play and indeed the whole of the play itself. In the same way, conductors can learn the whole of a complex score. It can also be seen that those who neglect to exercise their memory find it hard to remember even the shortest of texts, or to recall what they had previously memorized.

It can also be seen that memorization is easier when what is to be memorized has what is called in *Gestaltpsychologie* "good structure," a coherent and organized form. This is why poetry is easier to memorize than prose, and a melody easier than a random series of notes. In contrast, the content of the new media, especially the Internet, usually appears as a flow of motley elements with no inner coherence. Worse, with their hyperlinks and varied content, texts, photos, videos, and music, they act to disperse the mind.

For something to be memorized, it must be repeated many times with the same content and form of expression. In contrast, the new media constantly change what they show. On the Internet, pages pass by in a haphazard way while the television strives to avoid boring and losing its audience by treating what is static and repetitive as the worst of faults, and showing a series of clips as short as possible.

Memorizing something requires concentration and so to a lesser degree does recall. But as we shall see in the next section, using the new media weakens the ability to concentrate considerably. Anyone who has to deal with those dependent, even slightly, on the new media notices that there is often a delay before they answer a question: and sometimes they ask for the question to be repeated before answering. This is a sign that their short-term memory is degraded, like the degeneration encountered in sufferers of Alzheimer's disease or senility, but to a lesser extent. It is linked to absent-mindedness and to a lack of concentration.

Reflection and memory are closely linked as William James put it: "The art of remembering is the art of reflection."[216] There are also close links between memory and intelligence, for the intelligence structures the data provided by the senses and also by the memory. Weakening of the memory inevitably leads to weakening of reflection, thinking, and knowledge.

John Sweller, an educational psychologist has shown that two kinds of memory interact during learning: short-term memory and long-term memory. The first stores our immediate thoughts and impressions but only for a few seconds. The second stores everything we have learnt about the world, whether consciously or unconsciously, as long-term memories that may endure for days, months, years, or for the whole life. One form of short-term memory, the working memory, transfers information into the long-term memory and slowly builds up a personal knowledge base. At each instant, we are conscious only of the contents of the working memory. The short-term memory is like the note-pad of the mind whereas the long-term memory is its filing system. The long-term memory stores in an organized way facts, concepts, and designs. By referring to these, our thought makes sense of varied bits of information and becomes richer and deeper. The depth of our intelligence depends on our ability to transfer information from the working memory to the long-term memory and to integrate it into the conceptual patterns that we have developed over a long time.[217]

Unlike the long-term memory, which has a nearly limitless capacity, the working memory cannot hold very much information at any one time. What it holds soon disappears unless it is reactivated by repetition.

The transfer of information from the working memory to the long-term memory is like filling a bath tub with a thimble. The new media pour forth so much information so quickly that they have a big influence on this process. When we read a book, information flows through the faucet, drop by drop at a speed we can control by the speed of our reading. By concentrating on the text, we can transfer all or part of this information, a thimbleful at a time, into the long-term memory and create those rich connections that are essential for setting it in order. With the Internet we are faced with many information faucets, all of them gushing forth rapidly. Our little thimble overflows as we rush from one faucet to another. We can only transfer a tiny fraction of the information to our long-term memory and what we transfer is a patchwork of drops of information from different faucets and not a continuous and coherent flow from a single source.

The information that is held in our working memory at a given time can be called the "cognitive load." When this load exceeds the capacity of our mind to store and analyze the information—when the thimble overflows—we are no longer able to retain the information or to relate it to what is already stored in our long-term memory. We can no longer set the new information in order. Our ability to learn is reduced and our knowledge remains superficial. Experiments have shown that when we reach the limits of our working memory it becomes harder to distinguish between relevant and irrelevant information. We become dumb consumers of data.

The difficulty of understanding a subject or a concept can be seen to be "'heavily determined by working memory load,' writes Sweller, and the more complex the material we're trying to learn, the greater the penalty exacted by an overloaded mind." There are many causes of cognitive overload, but the two most important, according to Sweller, are solving external problems and dividing the attention. These two causes turn out to be two of the main characteristics of the Internet as a medium of information.[218]

Destroying the Capacity for Attention and Concentration

Another very serious effect of the new media on the life of the mind is the weakening, and even destruction, of the ability to attend and to concentrate. *Homo connecticus* is often incapable of sustained attention or concentration, or of sustaining an activity long enough to make it effective. As Raffaele Simone has said, "The media-sphere encourages flitting from one thing to another rather than concentrating, and fragmentation rather than continuity."[219]

Attention and concentration are closely linked: concentration requires attention and attention implies concentration. Attention means fixing and concentrating the consciousness for a certain time in one of its operations (perception, imagination, memory, reflection, etc.) on a particular object. Attention itself implies concentration as opposed to distraction or dispersion; and since it is fixed on its object, it is opposed to mobility and instability. Insofar as it requires a certain length of time, it is opposed to the instantaneous. Insofar as it works on a single task, it is opposed to performing several tasks at once.

However, the way the new media work and are used implies everything that is opposed to attention. As we have shown many times, they pour out a constant flow, moving and unstable, of texts, images, or sounds. When several functions are used at once, for example the computer and the smartphone, or the computer as workstation and email sender, this instability is increased by constantly switching the attention from one to the other. It goes without saying that the multiple signals emitted are permanent sources of distraction. There are the television's stream of images, the rings of the smartphone, the email alerts, the text messages, the tweets, the Facebook events, the news from the RSS flow and the rest, and the manifold temptations to distraction that they propose, zapping for the television, and hyperlinks for the Internet. Even when these things do not totally destroy attention, they stop it from working by turning it away from its object.

There are other factors that we have already discussed that take Internet users far beyond the sonorous alerts of their applications. Their desire to escape from loneliness or boredom and their constant search for novelty leads them to go out of themselves and continuously seek new messages. It becomes difficult for *homo connecticus* to find a timespan long enough to fix his attention and concentrate on something. He is overwhelmed by a world of outer and inner enticements that he cannot control. He is almost permanently interrupted and what time he has is of no duration. It is not made up of relatively long sequences but of a disordered succession of instants.

Then there is multitasking, simultaneously performing several tasks on different media: writing an email or consulting the Internet while making a phone call. This goes against the basic requirement of attention, which is to apply the consciousness to just one activity. Inevitably, attention is divided. This doesn't simply cut attention into two halves. Switching from one activity to another deprives each of them of the attention given to the other. Overall, this leads to an attention deficit for all the activities, each of which lacks the time of attention it needs to be properly done.[220] A further problem is that some of the overall attention is needed to manage the multitasking process, how to pass from one task to another, to forget the first, and attend to the next. So, there is less attention available for the tasks themselves. Multitasking also has a negative effect on the content of the consciousness itself. Those who practice it are more easily distracted than others by irrelevant enticements from their surroundings and can easily be distracted by almost anything.[221]

Attention is a capacity innate to mankind, but it is not mainly spontaneous, like perception. Like memory it is strengthened by practice and weakens when it is little used. The environment of the media encourages permanent distraction that prevents children from acquiring and developing a habit of attention and concentration, and destroys whatever force of attention and concentration an adult may have gained.[222]

One may say that to watch television requires a minimum of attention to follow the plot, and that using the Internet requires yet more since the navigator, the screen, and the content must all be managed or observed. This is why the Internet tires you out if you use it for too long. There is something to be said for these remarks, except that tiredness comes from the flow of information and from dispersion rather than from attention. To assess the value and the limits of this kind of attention, two types of attention must be distinguished, just as we distinguished two types of memory. There is passive attention and active attention.

Passive attention is not the beginning of active attention. It is neither a part of it nor a support for it. Instead, it opposes it. As one sees clearly with the television, passive attention captures all the attention and holds it captive. Indeed, this is one of the aims of television companies who employ most elaborate techniques to achieve this end,[223] leaving almost no space for active attention.

The user of the Internet is not passive before the screen like the watcher of television, dumb before the flow of images. He uses his mind to choose and define the content and his fingers to reach it; but part of his active attention is removed by this process. His passive attention allows itself to be captivated by the images, videos, sounds, and links that adorn the pages, whence comes the paradox referred to by Nicholas Carr: "Our use of the Internet involves many paradoxes, but the one that promises to have the greatest long-term influence over how we think is this one: the Net seizes our attention only to scatter it."[224]

The loss or weakening of the attention is very damaging to the ability of children to learn in school. Teachers see the effects in school. They notice how the students find it harder and harder to concentrate and instead are distracted and agitated. This began in the years when the young started to use intensely the new media: first television, then video games, computers, tablets, and smartphones. Hyperactivity is also becoming ever more common among the young of today. In certain countries, like Germany and the United States, it is considered as an illness and is widely treated with drugs like Ritaline; but it should be mainly attributed to the intensive use of the new media.

For adults a weakening of their capacity for attention can severely reduce the efficiency and quality of their work. The statistics show that a significant part of working time is taken up with activity on the new media. It is not always related to work, leading some businesses to take measures to prevent the use of private emails or smartphones when at work, and to forbid any use of the Internet not related to work.

The permanent enticements of the new media make work less efficient, more superficial, and multiply the chances of a mistake. This may have serious consequences in the case of operators of machine tools, drivers of vehicles, or medical professionals. In 2009, the *New York Times* published a series of articles about accidents caused by drivers being distracted by their smartphones. It would be easy to create a second series about what Americans call "distracted doctoring." An article in the same newspaper[225] expressed concern about this and gave several examples of it. There was a neurosurgeon who made personal phone calls through a hands-free kit during operations. There were anesthetists who surfed sites unrelated to work on the computers of the operating theater. There was a nurse buying airline tickets online with her iPhone during an operation. There were doctors and nurses looking at emails or sending them while they were inserting catheters into a patient. Finally, more than 50% of a sample of 439 hospital technicians would send text messages or make phone calls while monitoring the heart-lung bypass machine during heart surgery. Many medical professionals have been in the habit of multitasking for many years, and senior doctors have noticed that their junior colleagues are more liable to distraction since they have been trained to be permanently connected. "My firm conviction is that lives are in danger," wrote Dr. Papadakos who recently published an article in *Anesthesiology News* on "electronic distraction," which he described as "a digital nightmare."[226]

Fragmenting and Disorganizing Thought

One of the most catastrophic effects of using the new media is the fragmentation and disorganization of thought, which is largely the result of the dispersive processes we have just described: the television with its flow of changing images that the producers speed up all the time; the Internet with its succession of pages each with its sources of distraction; the various media used in real time; and multitasking, always switching the attention from one thing to another. All these disperse thought, making it lose its unity and coherence, if it ever had them, and preventing their acquisition by the young who are still learning. Even before these qualities are seriously degraded, the media change thought into a kind of patchwork of different materials, colors, and shapes not coherently bound together.

In a musical metaphor one could say that users of the Internet end up with a staccato corresponding to the way they switch between web pages,[227] giving a series of notes instead of a melody, bereft of any expression or legato.

Modifying the Structure of the Brain and the Way It Works

The argument of Nicholas Carr in *The Shallows* is that the Internet and the new media have changed in depth our way of thinking, and that this change has become imprinted on the structure and working of our brain. Before considering the Internet, he devotes a long chapter to show how scientific theories of the brain have evolved. It used to be thought that an adult's brain was stable with an almost unchanging structure, but, starting in the 1970s this has given way to the idea that the brain has a flexible and plastic structure even in adulthood.[228]

Every time we perform a task or feel a sensation whether they be physical or mental, a group of neurons in our brain is activated. If they are close to each other, the neurons link to each other by synaptic neurotransmitters. [...] If the same experience is repeated, the synaptic links between the neurons strengthen and multiply [...]. What we learn as we live is inscribed in our brain through ever-changing links between the cells. The circuits of neurons, linked together, are truly vital paths for our mind. Scientifically, the essential dynamics of neuronal plasticity are summed up in Hebb's Law: "Neurons that fire together, wire together."[229]

"Today," Carr continues, "the mists that have obscured the interplay between technology and the mind are beginning to lift. The recent discoveries about neuroplasticity ... tell us that the tools man has used to support or extend his nervous system—all those technologies that through history have influenced how we find, store, and interpret information, how we direct our attention and engage our senses, how we remember and how we forget—have shaped the physical structure and workings of the human mind. Their use has strengthened some neural circuits and weakened others, reinforced certain mental traits while leaving others to fade away."[230]

Among the new technologies, it is without doubt those of the new media, which are linked to the Internet, that have made the greatest contribution to remodeling the structure and working of the human brain. Their use takes up much time in the life of modern man. They actively engage his different mental and intellectual powers (sensations and movements of the upper members), and imply repetitive phenomena on the mental and motor planes. Carr writes of this:

"One thing is very clear," he writes: "If, knowing what we do today about the brain's plasticity, you were to set out to invent a medium that would rewire our mental circuits as quickly and thoroughly as possible, you would probably end up designing something that looks and works a lot like the Internet... . With the exception of alphabets and number systems, the Net may well be the single most powerful mind-altering technology that has ever come into general use. At the very least, it's the most powerful that has come along since the book."[53]

We know that the working and structure of our brain is changed significantly each time we learn a new skill. So, we can imagine what repercussions those activities linked to the new media may have. Repeated many times every day they end up by having the same effect as millions of training sessions. Our brains cannot but be "massively remodeled by this exposure."[232]

It is important to realize that the neurological effects on our brain arise not only from what we do when we used the new media but also by what is left out when we use them. Nicholas Carr explains:

> Just as neurons that fire together wire together, neurons that don't fire together don't wire together. As the time we spend scanning Web pages crowds out the time we spend reading books, as the time we spend exchanging bite-sized text messages crowds out the time we spend composing sentences and paragraphs, as the time we spend hopping across links crowds out the time we devote to quiet reflection and contemplation, the circuits that support those old intellectual functions and pursuits weaken and begin to break apart. The brain recycles the disused neurons and synapses for other more pressing work. We gain new skills and perspectives but lose old ones.[55]

Certainly, it is not the brain that defines the content of thought, for this has its source in the human spirit; but in the present state of the human being, the soul and body are related and interact. The form of our thought helps to mold our brain. In return, our brain, through the neuronal circuits created by our habits of thought, of action or reaction, orients the ways and workings of our thought.

The flow of various and disconnected pieces of information that the new media pour forth, the host of enticements that disperse and distract the activity of our mental powers, weakening attention and reducing concentration, the habit of reading diagonally, of writing in abbreviations all imprint themselves on the brain as habits and normal ways of working for *homo connecticus*. He reacts spontaneously in this way not only online but in everyday life, in every situation, so his whole way of life is deeply affected.

In the end, the new media bring forth a new man. This is a fact of which the large media companies are well aware, Google for instance, which finances research in the field of the trans-human.

CHAPTER 12

The Impoverishment of Spiritual Life

> Only when we have their attention can we hope
> to win their hearts and minds.
> —Eric Schmidt, former CEO of Google

The new media have, in the same way, led to the impoverishment of spiritual life. More and more, they have taken the place of traditional religions and spiritual practices, and at the same time they are changing and partly destroying the inner and outer conditions that favor the practice and development of spiritual life.

The Rising of a New Religion

It is clear to everyone that the world of the media has become a breeding ground for new spiritual practices and new religions. The new media are seen as a way to a new world and a new man, the ideal of all religions. The adoption of the new media by the people is preached for reasons that go beyond the commercial aim of selling devices, software, and applications, and the political aim of boosting the economy. Using them is said to bring many benefits for the personal development of the individual, the strengthening of the bonds of society, and the well-being and life of the population. Just as a television in every home was once seen as a sign of the progress of civilization, so the general use of computers and the Internet from the earliest age, and the possession of a smartphone by everyone on the planet are now seen as great advances. The new media are presented as the basic condition for the blossoming and happiness of modern man. They are said to open the door to a future full of promise and the emergence of humanity enhanced.

The sociologist Philippe Breton is one of those who has demonstrated the religious character of the new media in his essays: *L'Utopie de la communication*[234] and especially *Le Culte de l'Internet*. In the introduction to this second work he writes:

> The infatuation with the internet spreads in a climate which truly seems to be that of a new religion. This becomes clearer and clearer when one draws near to the circles which are its most ardent proselytes[235].

The religious character of the new media has been noted by other writers. Armand Mattelart sees a religious dimension in Marshall McLuhan's exaltation of the "global village."[236] Ignacio Ramonet fears that the technologies of communication may evolve into a "messianism of the media."[237] David Le Breton shows that there is a link between the religiosity of cyber-culture and the Gnosticism of the early Christian Era[238]. Mark Dery shows the link between American cyber-culture and the spiritualist New Age movement[239]. Pierre Musso gives the following critique of the networks: "A new god arises, a technical god. The internet is just one of his luminous apparitions: The Net. Everywhere the image of the Net prevails to enchant daily life and reinterpret the contemporary world. It is the idol of the contemporary cult of movement, of flow and of connection, linking the present to the future." According to him the great networks of today are "'the modern cathedrals of flow,' which no longer reach out to heaven but are at once the theatres of a movement toward a better world and of setting the present in perpetual motion."[240] Philippe Breton sees this new spirituality as a religion without a god. It has its roots in Gnosticism, in Manicheism, in dualism, in the counter-culture of the 1960s when the New Age embraced the spirituality of the Far East, and in the theology of Teihard de Chardin, which proposes to end the divisions among men by promoting the noosphere[241].

In *The Shallows*, Nicholas Carr devotes a chapter to "The Church of Google,"[242] and there have since been many articles that attest to the close links of Google to the transhumanist movement. The religious dimension of this partnership of the most important organizer of the Internet and the new media is obvious.

Philippe Breton shows how the religious character of the new media was already well developed at the dawn of IT, then called cybernetics, in Norbert Wiener's work. Starting in 1942, he developed his ideas and summed them up in his famous work *The Human Use of Human Beings*.[243] Wiener proposes that communication should be recognized as the fundamental value for man and society around which he constructs a unified and all-embracing vision of the world. The idea of entropy has a central role. It suggests that the world tends toward a state of maximum disorder that could threaten man himself and the relations established between communities. Wiener sees this not simply as an evil, but as the work of the Devil. According to him, only communication can counteract this tendency. Man can only find salvation by becoming a communicating being, and machines for communication are needed for him to achieve this end. For this reason, they are good: they oppose evil. The new man imagined by Wiener no longer expresses his worth through his own activity, but through his social interactions. According to Wiener, man can only be understood as a communicating being. In this idea of Wiener, Philippe Breton sees not simply a utopia, but a real theology that is the basis for a religious anthropology: a new society and a new man emerge from the victory of good (communication) over evil (entropy).[244]

This new religion of Wiener's was not adopted and the idea of entropy on which his system was based has now been forgotten. But Wiener rightly prophesied the central place of communication in the future. It rapidly invaded every area of human existence, both social and personal: the economy, politics, culture, science, literature, religion, education, work and leisure. He also prophesied the coming of *homo communicans*, entirely defined by his connections, and thus becoming *homo connecticus*, sacrificing a great part of his time and energy to the new cult and its rites linked to the use of the new media and the social networks.

Over the last 40 or 50 years there have been many books and articles exalting the virtues of the new media in mystical and prophetic terms. A typical example is the work of the Canadian philosopher, Pierre Lévy, *World philosophie*.[245] The new world made up of the new media is presented as an ideal world, peaceful and unified, where everyone becomes better informed and more aware. They thus become more intelligent and create positive relationships with each other. Boundaries and compartment disappear and make the world a village full of "friends" and humanity one big family.

Through the continuity of the new media, and especially of connected objects, the plan of a new man unfurls. He is to be freed from his present limitations, reprogrammed and augmented, thanks to the techniques of bionics, robotics, and IT, which in synergy he perfects. He gains limitless memory and a supremely powerful artificial intelligence. Thus, he acquires the divine qualities of omnipotence over himself and the environment, of incorruptibility and immortality.

Those who promote human enhancement and transhumanism[246] of which it is part are clearly the heirs of the American cyber-culture of the 1980s. They benefit from strong ideological and financial support from the large companies that have developed IT, the Internet, and connected objects, especially Google and its subsidiaries. The religious character of this movement, which is strongly anchored in North American culture, has been emphasized. It also has a sectarian side to it, having the totalitarian aim of world-wide development and influence over states and their citizens. This is seen, for example, in the World Transhumanist Association founded by David Pearce and Nick Bostrom, which is now called Humanity.

A Religion Without Ethics

It should not be thought that this new religion is a disinterested philanthropic project. The promised incorruptibility and immortality are not free gifts of grace, but products: the companies that finance these projects clearly plan to profit from any discoveries of ways to improve the health of humans and to prolong their lives. Those who are to be saved are those who can pay. Those who are to be damned are those who cannot. This has led some to fear that society will develop into two levels: the level of supermen (enhanced humans) and the level of sub-men, deprived of the enhancement of the supermen.

This new religion is also without morals or ethics: anything that can be achieved technically is not only permitted but desirable, and anything that pays is good. At first, Google adopted the motto: "Don't' be evil!," which itself shows a certain distance from what is good; but nowadays the company hardly ever considers such things. The ex-CEO, Eric Schmidt, commented cynically on this motto: "Now, when I showed up, I thought this was the stupidest rule ever, because there's no book about evil except maybe, you know, the Bible or something."

A New Cult

The transhumanist associations have developed mainly in the United States, and it is from there that they hope to conquer the world. In spite of their mainly atheist and humanist ethos they portray themselves as substitutes for Christianity. One can find in them the ideal of Christian perfection expressed in the patristic doctrine of the divinization of man[247], and moreover, the ideal of a "new man" who will put off the "old man," which echoes St Paul's expressions in the epistle to the Colossians 3:9–10. Yet these ideals are transposed from the spiritual level to the material level, and are to be brought about not by the Grace of the all-powerful God but by the promethean force of man, helped by the technologies he has invented to conquer nature.

At a more modest level, the new media have been glorified and exalted from the beginning in books and articles and this has produced a cult of their veneration. This cult is not just theoretical since in practice many users give the new media a central place in their lives: the place that God should occupy in the normal religious life of the faithful. They give them much time; they sacrifice their strength to them; they give up many things for them in what resembles a kind of detachment. Like ascetics, they give up food, and especially sleep, in their service and begin and end the day with them, just like religious folk with their morning and evening prayers.[248]

Often, the use of the new media, especially the Internet, replaces certain religious offices, even in monastic circles; and as ecclesiastical institutions develop the use of new media to strengthen links or as new means of evangelization, they strengthen a virtual spirituality to the detriment of real spiritual life.

A recent scientific study has demonstrated a correlation between the development of the new media and the abandonment of religion, or at least religious practice. In North America and Europe, it is Christianity that mainly suffers.[249] There are doubtless other factors that explain why more and more forsake Christianity in the West: secular society and the development of materialism and individualism. There is also the way the Christian message has been weakened in the second half of the twentieth century. In an attempt to bring it closer to the people it also has been strongly secularized, and for the sake of Ecumenism, it has been watered down and deprived of part of its identity. However, the new media have a power of attraction that consumes people's time and distracts them from traditional activities and from the world round them; and in this way they have undoubtedly contributed to this disenchantment with Christianity.

The Limits of Online Religious Practice

All sectors of society are present in the new media, so it is perhaps impossible for religions to be absent. This would leave the space free for others and would deprive them of a way of reaching the greater part of humanity who are all now connected. At first, religions had a small presence on certain television channels, but have since spread out on the web with information sites, blogs, and various discussion sites. They have also produced various applications for smartphones.

In this way, religious communities can reach out beyond their membership to any connected person who may come across them by chance and who otherwise would not have been aware of their existence. So, the Internet seems to be a great tool for mission and preaching. It is also a means of obtaining information and various other resources, and a place where the lonely can find company. But those who use the web for religious ends should temper their enthusiasm. For as we have shown in previous chapters there are problems, and the web has its limits.

Each administrator or blogger tends to see his blog as the center of the web. He forgets that for a potential reader it is just one among the 200 million on the web, or one among the million religious blogs. By looking at the religious blogs it can be seen that all religions compete on the web as well as all kinds of sects. For some of them, the Internet has become a propaganda tool. Recent events have shown how Islamic sites, skillfully crafted to indoctrinate and manipulate minds, have managed to recruit people to fight in the Middle East and sacrifice their lives. Those who went were not only young Muslims seeking a radical ideal, but young folk who had never been in contact with Islam and who met convincing persuaders by chance on the web.

In general, the sects have a much greater presence on the web than in other media, which rarely give them space. On the web, expression is entirely free and uncontrolled and allows the sects to reach a public far greater those around them. Often their members have the zeal of new converts and use it in proselytism.

It is possible to profit from a chance encounter with a good quality religious site, but in general, the sites of traditional religions only attract those who are already in tune with what they represent. In that case the problems that have already been identified arise: rapid, superficial diagonal reading, distraction of the mind by links and images. Worse, they encourage a virtual relationship with the institution.

A Christian service or Mass watched on the television or the Internet by a lonely person may be useful and beneficial, but the virtual video is far from the reality itself. Watching is an individual experience, not the communal experience of the Liturgy, which in Greek is called the *synaxis*, meaning assembly. The communion between persons and Eucharistic Communion that are inherent in the Liturgy are also impossible. Moreover, the production team treats the Mass as a show, and the result has the same faults, though less marked, as an ordinary show, where changing camera angles successively presents the spectator with different viewpoints and disperses his mind.

A Poor Substitute for Confession

As we have already seen, the new media have eliminated the boundary between private and public life and have encouraged the exposure of intimacy to the most immodest degree. Sometimes this is unconscious, as when we speak loudly on the phone in public. Sometimes it is willful, as when we recount our intimate lives and states of mind on blogs and discussion forums. These can be substitutes for the psychoanalyst's couch, which itself, for many years, has been a substitute for the confessional.[250]

Such an exposure of one's intimate life undoubtedly has a liberating effect at a psychological level: an emotional release.[251] But far from placing one's ego at a distance, as would a confession or psychoanalysis, it usually serves to place the ego at the center. This, as Christopher Lasch has shown, fits perfectly into the "culture of narcissism," which is the mark of modern societies.[252] All this is clearly far from the sacrament of Christian confession, where the penitent recalls his sins, his faults, and his failings so as to repent, which means changing his conduct. The priest gives him the absolution that wipes away past failings and gives strength to do better in future.

In certain countries, especially in the United States, Christian confession online or by telephone has been tried. While this practice brings the benefits that come from openness and listening it can hardly be seen as a sacrament. Like all sacraments, confession implies a real, face-to-face relationship with the priest, and also certain rites whose material and sensory character are absolutely essential.[253]

Substituting the Horizontal for the Vertical

We have emphasized the religious character, in the broad sense, of the new media, but this is a religion without God and spirituality without Spirit. Transhumanism itself is another form of humanism, based on the humanism of the Renaissance, which sets man in the place of God. It rests on the enlightenment of the eighteenth century that replaced the facts of the Revelation with the speculations of the reason and on scientism, which sees scientific knowledge as the highest form of knowledge. It places its hope in scientific discovery, to ensure the perfecting and happiness of humanity, and in technicism, which sees technical development as the standard of human progress.

Alain Finkielkraut observes correctly that with the new technologies: "we abandon a world of contemplation and reaching upwards and enter a world of openness and reaching sideways."[254] As we use the Internet, we see how its web spreads horizontally, and how the movement of the spirit that moves within it is one of permanent alienation.

Technology That Bears the Seal of "This World"

Father Constantine Coman, a professor of the Theological Faculty of Bucharest, wrote recently that the new media are an invention of this world. They are fertile ground for those worldly attitudes that a spiritual man flees as he seeks "the one thing needful" in depth. For they bring forth distraction, pleasure seeking, levity, curiosity, talkativeness, and empty gossip.[255] The new media also go ever faster, like much in the modern world, and unlike traditional societies that slow down so as better to contemplate mankind and the world.

This rapidity goes with ceaseless movement, a permanent quest for change and the instability that marks the modern world—the opposite of the stability that is cultivated by the Liturgy and personal spirituality. The constant quest for change, not spiritual progress, is on the whole a bad sign: it suggests permanent dissatisfaction since when we like something, we do not wish to change it but to cling on to it.

Man, Riveted to Matter and the Body by the Internet and Connected Objects

Large numbers of Internet connections are linked to the consumption of material goods. This makes it very useful to business. It brings immense profits, not just to the sites that sell, but also to the sites that collect personal data, which can be re-sold for commercial exploitation. The new media have encouraged the spirit of consumerism by showing the consumer more desirable goods than he could ever see in a traditional store, and feeding his lust to acquire them. The Internet has become the main instrument of a cult that, for more than half a century, many philosophers have called "the religion of consumption."[256]

Connected objects have allowed the new media to go further, toward a cult of matter and the body. Their purpose is almost always to give man effortless power at a distance over the objects that surround him. Many of these connected objects are also related to sport, or to the supposed well-being of the body. They are almost always measuring devices designed to help improve physical performance. They are part of the cult of the body and youthfulness, which marks modern Western Civilization, where sport has also become a kind of religion.

Communication: A Substitute for Communion

Through emails, text messages, and social networks, the new media are credited with helping to forge relations between humans, and even, especially through Facebook, to give them friendship. As we have seen, to connect each individual to everyone else was one of the aims of the utopian society imagined by Wiener in a semi-religious way. One might think that these ideas are at one with modern personalist philosophy as found in Judaism (Buber, Lévinas), or Catholicism (Mounier), or even Orthodoxy (Berdiaev, Yannaras, Zizioulas), where a person is defined as a being in relation to others, the relationship being the only way this can come about.

But as we saw in a preceding chapter, the relationships that are created through the new media are very superficial. The so-called friends of Facebook, gained at the click of a mouse, are friends but in name. It is risky to reduce one's neighbor to a Facebook "friend" or a Twitter "follower." As Peter Pilt has shown, this replaces the love of one's neighbor, which always implies concrete action along with effort and sacrifice, with "likes" produced by the simple click of a mouse. In this way, Christianity is replaced by what he calls "Clickstianity."[257] Pilt emphasizes that there is a similar risk in confusing activity on the social networks with spirituality. A cartoon shows a man who has just died arriving in Heaven. When God asks him: "What did you do with your life?," he replies with surprise: "What! Didn't you read my tweets?"

We have shown that relationships created by the new media have a virtual dimension. They are abstract, bodiless, lacking depth, and complexity. The nuances and all the visual and emotional richness of concrete relationships are lacking. Even those connections where the faces are present on screen cannot provide the feeling of a real presence. This is shown by the remark that users of Skype often make without realizing: "I miss you!"

Paradoxically, such relationships can be formed between lonely individuals who have never met, and often, who would never want to meet for fear of exposure or disappointment. The social media tend to replace real communities with virtual communities. Some are happy with this change[258], but it is clear that the virtual, by its very nature, has not the human or spiritual density of the concrete.

In fact communication has become a substitute for communion, which, in its spiritual reality, rests on the participation in one Body and one Spirit in a concrete community[259].

A Connection Competing with Connection to God

The facts show that connection to the new media competes with connection to God, which is made through participation in Liturgical services and through personal prayer. As we have said many times, the new media eat up time. The television does so and even more so the Internet. Through its links it entices the user to navigate further and further, capturing his attention and making him forget the passage of time. Anyone who has used the Internet has often found that a search that should have been quick took far longer than intended.

In this competition between connections, the new media win hands down. In spite of all the love we may have for Him, to connect with God we must make an effort to withdraw from our environment and from our own thoughts in the widest sense (reasoning, imagination, memories, desires, etc.) and be vigilant and attentive; navigating the Internet is easy. It is enough to let oneself go to plunge into a pleasant world that always assuages our desires and passions. Moreover, there is a sense of total freedom, whereas to relate to God within the framework of serious and sincere religious practice implies permanent regularity and discipline.

The monasteries themselves have managed to escape the invasion of the television, but find it harder to resist the new media. More and more monks, for various more or less valid reasons, now have access to a computer. More and more of them have a portable phone, which nowadays is a device that includes all the other media. In a coenobitic monastery, the rule may forbid or limit the use of portable media; but solitaries escape such control. Many hermits pass time on the Internet that could better have been given to prayer, and many monks spy through that small window every day on the world that they left through the front door.

The Many and Varied Sources of Temptation

The new media are always a temptation to turn from the task in hand, and also from our neighbor, our own spiritual benefit, and from God Himself. The Internet is a constant source of temptations. It is not just a device to escape boredom or to hide in a virtual world believed to be more gratifying than reality, but is a door open to the objects of every desire and passion.

Temptations always present themselves spontaneously to man, and this is also the way with the Internet. It shows texts, links, and especially images, providing as one navigates suggestions without number, and often unexpected. For the companies that manage the Internet organize it so that the user sees as much as possible of everything to which he is easily tempted.

Provoking and Feeding the Passions

If we review the basic list of all the passions, compiled by Eastern Christian Tradition to guide man in his spiritual progress, we can see that there is not one to which the new media cannot tempt us, and that they cannot arouse, feed, maintain, or develop. They are as follows: love of the belly, or gluttony; avarice, or the love of money and the desire to acquire more money and goods; lust, or attachment to sexual pleasure; anger, which includes all forms of aggression; fearfulness, which includes disquiet and anxiety; sadness; acedia, the state of dissatisfaction, disgust, laziness, and instability; self-love, vanity or vainglory; and pride[260].

The television itself incites these passions. It shows a huge number of programs with violent[261] or sexual[262] content. It has also started to show temptations to gluttony with programs dedicated to cooking, to cake baking and bakers, to chocolate and chocolate makers, all of which are most successful. By multiplying the number of programs about consumption, it helps to place the spectators in the material world where all this takes place. By indulging in programs that describe how the rich live in luxury, it develops avarice. Through a whole range of movies and soaps that are full of scenes of violence, it develops aggression in those who watch them[263]. Through violent horror movies and dramatic and alarming documentaries, it is an important factor in the development of fearfulness, disquiet, and anxiety[264]. The situation is made worse by the hundreds of channels devoted to sex, gambling, cooking, and to all the vanities of the world that have been freely available for 30 or 40 years.

As for the Internet, it offers the same wares as the television plus all possible kinds of content through texts, sounds, photos, or videos. It allows any temptation to be followed up easily, an object to be found for any desire, a development for any fantasy, and food for any passion.

We have already mentioned certain sites that encourage behavior contrary to the respect and love due to one's neighbor. Besides the sites devoted to speaking ill and slander (like Gossip), the ordinary forums and discussion groups found on the Internet encourage the same bad behavior along with verbal aggression that is facilitated by the generalized use of pseudonyms.

Self-exposure and Overexposure: A New Terrain for the Practice of Self-love, Vanity, and Pride

The television has strongly encouraged the desire for media exposure, not only among those in public life (actors, singers, and politicians) but also among ordinary folk, fascinated by the fame that comes from simply taking part in a television program. The Internet, through YouTube and Facebook, allows anyone to show movies of his most trivial words and actions to a huge mass of users, or to boast about his wildest behavior, his absurd and even suicidal exploits.

The social networks, such as Facebook and Twitter, and the discussion blogs and forums encourage self-exposure and even over-exposure. Many users of the Internet blithely describe their most trivial acts. They emit a stream of consciousness carrying their impressions, sentiments, and thoughts of the moment in complete disorder. Through videos and photos they expose their personal and family life without the least modesty or reserve. This reveals their desire to attract the attention of others to themselves. It manifests the narcissism that we have already described. One of its main expressions is the *selfie*, a photo of oneself taken with a smartphone, which is contemplated, as in a mirror, or posted on the social networks before the public gaze. How strange that these postings of photos or videos on the social networks should be called "sharing," when they are acts based on egotism, linked to vanity and pride. This attitude is reinforced by what follows when the success of these "shares" is judged by the number of "likes" they attract.

What might be seen in a child as a means of learning to become conscious of his personal existence is in an adult an expression of untamed primary narcissism. Long before Freud, the holy ascetics of the Christian East identified this behavior and gave it the name of "philautism," or egotistical love of self.[265] They considered it to be a deep-seated passion, the mother of all the others, like vanity and pride with which it is closely linked, and which are also among the worst passions. Hiding behind ideas of "communication" and "sharing" makes them even worse, for it gives them a false appearance of altruism.

Pride and vanity are reinforced by counting the "likes" received, and by showing that one can collect more *followers* on Twitter, or "likes" from the so-called friends of Facebook than the next man. Those who use Facebook tend to show a flattering image of themselves, which surpasses reality. Their faults are erased and their qualities exaggerated. They even claim qualities that they never had. This has a bad effect not just on themselves, but on others who may feel put down by the outrageous exaggeration they see in the images that they take to be true. Psychologists have even found that it is a cause of depression, which concords with the teaching of the holy ascetics who saw pride and vanity as sources of sadness and acedia, two states that resemble what we now call depression.[266]

The new media have found their place in that modern Western culture that Christopher Lasch called "the culture of narcissism."[267] They have strongly encouraged its development, opposing the Christian culture of self-effacement through modesty and humility and esteem of one's neighbor through charity and love.

An Unfailing Source of Distraction and Entertainment

As we showed in the previous chapter, the new media are a source of distraction and entertainment, far beyond anything known in the past, since they can be permanent and limitless. Formerly, someone who sought entertainment had to make a physical and psychological effort to move to the right place and pay the price demanded. The television and Internet bring it all into the home offering a huge choice that requires no effort of any kind to be accessed. Moreover, communications through the Internet and smartphones, emails, text messages, tweets and Facebook alerts, require the permanent attention of *homo connecticus*, turning him away from himself and from God toward external objects that may be virtual or (half) real but are always worldly.

Destroyers of *Hesychia*

The new media destroy what the Eastern Spiritual Tradition refers to as *hesychia*. In truth, this state can only be lived to the full by monastics. Yet all who would lead a serious spiritual life need it in some measure. *Hesychia* is a way of life that requires solitude, outer silence, and inner calm. These three things are indispensable for spiritual life, especially in one of its essential activities: concentrated attentive and vigilant prayer. In contrast, the continual prompts from the new media are incompatible with the creation and maintenance of *hesychia*, not only in its fullness but also for even the briefest periods. It has no chance against the visual and audible signals to which most connected people respond immediately.

Replacement of Inner Stability by Ceaseless Movement and Disturbance

Hesychia is also a state of inner stability that is required for prayer and that is strengthened by it. At its higher levels, spiritual life aims for inner peace that is not merely the absence of psychological disturbance, but also that absence of spiritual trouble, which is the fruit of the quenching of the passions. This is the first aim of the ascetic life in that stage of spiritual life that Eastern Christian Tradition calls *praxis*.

Even when it does not rise to this level, spiritual life requires and cultivates stability in life, and to this end gives great importance to regularity, which comes from discipline and contributes to the mastery of all the faculties.

The effects of the new media are quite the opposite of this state. As we have seen, using them often gives rise to disquiet that increases with use, or to dissatisfaction that the user seeks to assuage by always seeking something new. They drag all the powers of the soul into a continuous fast-flowing stream of disordered and disconnected impressions. Their content arouses desire, provokes fears, and develops the passions, which are so many sources of every kind of trouble for the soul.

Replacing Recollection by Dispersion

Spiritual life also requires what is traditionally called recollection, the capacity to turn all one's faculties inward, away from the world, there in one's heart to unite and consecrate them to God in meditation and prayer. Recollection is the stage of preparation for prayer that precedes concentration. But as we have seen, the new media push man's faculties in the opposite sense, always outwards toward the world. They are dispersed by a stream of discordant nagging that cuts the soul in pieces, and destroys the unity and identity of the inner man[268].

The new media encourage strongly two elements of ancestral sin:[269] (1) the loss of the inner unity of the faculties, which once were united in knowledge of God and doing His Will, dispersing them among physical objects and their representations (thoughts, memories, and images), or the desires and passions that they arouse; (2) the resulting division, chopping up, and inner dispersion,[270] which, according to St Maximus the Confessor, "breaks human nature into a thousand fragments."[271] As other holy ascetics have said, the intelligence is then constantly distracted,[272] floating, erring, and wandering here and there[273] in a state of permanent agitation,[274] quite the opposite of the deep peace it experienced in its former contemplation. The thoughts that once were united and concentrated become manifold and multifarious, spreading out in a ceaseless flow.[275] They divide and disperse,[276] leaking out in every direction,[277] dragging and dividing the whole being of man in their wake. This leads St Maximus the Confessor to speak of: "the scattering of the soul amongst outer forms according to the appearance of sensory things,"[278] for the soul becomes multiple in the image of this sensory multiplicity that, paradoxically, she has created for herself, and which is simply an illusion arising from her incapacity to perceive the objective unity of beings through her ignorance of their relation to the One God in their origins and their end.

Once the intelligence becomes dispersed and divided among the swarm of thoughts and sensations that it has engendered, all the faculties follow. Stirred up and excited by a multitude of passions, they pull in many directions, often opposed, at once, and make of man a being divided at every level. This process of the fall of man, described by the Church Fathers of Late Antiquity, continues today faster than ever, driven on by the new media. They offer such a rich and speedy flow of temptations that they multiply the sensory objects that attract the senses and all man's faculties; and they increase the dispersion and division that arises when man's faculties are attached to them.

The Negative Effect on Vigilance and Attention, Two Essential Foundations of Spiritual Life

Although he starts from a viewpoint different from that of the Church Fathers, Matthew Crawford writes in his recent book of distraction as "the original sin of the spirit." He emphasizes that attention, on the contrary, is one of man's most precious faculties. It does not just contribute to all his various activities, but brings about his inner unity, preserving his identity in the face of the outer world. Crawford's philosophical and psychological views concord with the warning of Deuteronomy 4:9: "Take heed to yourself and diligently guard your soul," and with Christ's many injunctions to his Apostles to keep vigilance (Matthew 24:42; 25:13; 26:41; Mark 13:33,37; 14:38; Luke 21:36), and with the recommendations of the Apostles themselves (Acts 20:28; 1 Corinthians 16:13; 1 Peter 5:8). They also agree with the age-old teachings of hesychasm, the most elaborate form of Orthodox Spirituality: attention is essential to the effectiveness and development of spiritual life. St Peter of Damascus goes so far as to teach: "Without attention and vigilance of spirit we cannot be saved and delivered from the devil, who, as a roaring lion, walketh about us, seeking whom he may devour."[279] To establish a solid and fruitful relationship with God and build himself up spiritually, a Christian must be attentive to himself. He needs a permanent attitude of vigilance (*nepsis*) to avoid evil thoughts (including diverting thoughts) and must remain attentive to God in undistracted prayer so as to develop a solid and fruitful relationship with God, which also builds him up spiritually by uniting him with the One God. St Niketas Stethatos writes: "Whilst we are divided by the fickleness of thoughts and the law of the flesh rules and endures within us, we are dispersed amongst the many parts which make us up and we are rejected far from Divine Unity, for we have not drawn on the riches of this unity."[280]

The notions of vigilance and unity are two matters that are mentioned many times in the *Philokalia*, an anthology prepared in Greece in the eighteenth century by St Nikodemos the Hagiorite and St Macarius of Corinth. A Slavonic version was later prepared by St Paisius Velichkovsky and a Russian one by St Theophan the Recluse. It is a collection of the most important texts on spiritual life from the Fathers of the fourth to fourteenth centuries and is a major reference work for Orthodox Spirituality. It is significant that the full title of this collection is the *Philokalia of the neptic Fathers*, that is to say, the vigilant Fathers. Certain classics of hesychast spirituality include the words "vigilance" or "attention" in their title. Here are some examples: *On vigilance and guarding the heart* by St Nikephoros the Solitary,[281] *Chapters on vigilance* by St Hesychius of Batos (Mt Sinai),[282] or the famous *Method of holy prayer and attention* formerly attributed to St Symeon the New Theologian.[283] As St Nikephoros the Solitary writes, the notions of attention (*prosokhe*), vigilance (*nepsis*), sobriety (another meaning of *nepsis*), and *hesychia* are very close and all describe the same attitude.[284]

CHAPTER 13

Prevention and Treatment

Let us break their bonds asunder, and cast away their cords from us.
—Psalm 2:3

The main aim of this work is to diagnose the different pathologies provoked by the new media in the hope of showing the scale of the problem to those who have been blinded by the general elation that has come with these developments. To know the different forms of the sickness and their causes is clearly an essential stage in their cure.

The above analyses will doubtless help folk to draw back to a healthy distance. They will have understood that in this lie the main forms of treatment and prevention. As far as possible, one must abstain from the use of the new media and regulate what use one makes of them by self-limitation. In this way, one may escape as far as possible from their negative effects.

Total abstinence is without doubt the best. To achieve this requires a struggle to bring about another kind of society, another world. For it is clear from all we have said that the new media have sprung up like weeds in the soil of a civilization that has become worldwide, and is based on the myths of progress and the excessive value placed on technical development. Its aim is the limitless increase of profits for its main participants, the multinationals whose power has surpassed that of nation states. Given the dynamics of its present development, the possibility of a fundamental change of direction is far off. Our world is so organized that it is extremely hard to abstain entirely from the new media. Realistically, we must compromise. We can limit our use of the new media to what is essential for our way of life, especially for our work. This may seem a rather modest goal, but if more and more people were to act in this way, the desired decline of these media would at least begin. When the ship sinks, there is no point in dreaming of a calmer sea and a better vessel. Lives must be saved. When one reaches the shore, safe and sound, one can begin to plan for the longer term. So in this last chapter, we will restrict ourselves to suggesting simple and practical remedies.

How to Cure Dependency

Many users of the new media have become dependent on them, or at least one of them, such as the television, the Internet, or the mobile phone. They may also be dependent on a cyber-assisted habit, such as gaming, pornography, or compulsive purchasing.

Sometimes this dependency is not recognized as such by the subject as it is part of his existence, a way of life. It may be recognized by those close to the subject who themselves suffer because of it. It may also finally be recognized by the subject himself when he starts to suffer socially as his relations to others are disturbed, or psychologically through the ungovernable impulses and frustrations he feels, or physically through tiredness and nervous exhaustion. Different treatments are indicated as a function of the degree of dependency.

Psychotherapy

As we have seen, dependency on the new media is similar to dependency on drugs. So in severe cases, psychotherapy is needed with psychiatrists specialized in addictions.[285] This is all the more necessary when the patient has gone as far as burn out, with its intense physical and psychological exhaustion that may lead to a syndrome of depression. The problem has developed and lengthy treatments are needed. In America and China, where the problem is more severe than in Europe, clinics have been created specialized in the detox of those addicted to the new media. They are similar to those specialized in alcohol or drugs and provide lengthy and continuous treatment in an isolated environment.[286]

The basic method of detox is to wean the patient from his addiction. He is cut off from all contact with the new media in a safe space under surveillance. A total rupture can be achieved since in this case, unlike dependency on drugs, there are no undesirable physical reactions. In the United States there are more and more cases of dependent patients who have undergone such treatment for periods of up to a year. However, it must be realized that addiction to the Internet and other new media, like addiction to drugs, is at first "a solution" before it becomes a problem. It is a response to existential problems that are at its root and that must also be treated urgently. Otherwise the effect of addiction therapy will just be temporary. These existential problems most often arise from deep spiritual roots and so require a spiritual therapy.

Some Guidelines for Less Severe Cases

Not all the forms of addiction to the new media are grave enough to need a stay in hospital, or even psychotherapy. The firm intention to reduce exposure or simply to avoid the worst of the consequences described in previous chapters can bring those concerned to take measures to control themselves. These can be effective if there is personal discipline.[287]

Retreats

More and more of those intoxicated by the new media realize that they are in a troubling psychological and physical state. They often have a strong enough will to take radical measures and cut themselves off for a certain time from all sorts of connected devices. In the press, there are more and more reports of the positive results of such long-term retreats.[288]

Those who cannot cut themselves off completely for so long, often for professional reasons, are advised to unplug regularly for short periods of at least five days. This radical interruption of all types of connection brings psychological and physical rest. It also allows, at least partially, the diverted and weakened connections in the brain to be regenerated and restructured. In the United States there is a National Unplugging Day each year. This is certainly not long enough, but at least recalls, symbolically, the need to disconnect from time to time. There are also groups that imitate the sexual abstinence movement, which has become fashionable to the West of the Atlantic. The members of these groups of digital abstainers[289] support each other in their efforts to unplug for times of various durations. *Digital detox*, which started as a movement in Silicon Valley, has now spread to the hotels: spa hotels[290] and thalassotherapy centers have added digital detox to their menus.[291]

Unplugging from Media That Are Not Really Needed

Social and economic conditioning, ever-present imitation, and conformity make all social media seem indispensable, but in reality few of them are. In some families, people live fine with no television. It is also perfectly possible to live without Facebook or Twitter. Some have cancelled their accounts and feel the better for it. Other media, like the Internet or the smartphone, have become indispensable for certain administrative or commercial operations. However, in the private domain, it is possible to limit strictly their use through filters, and more especially by programming periods when they are disconnected.

Following the recent scandal of Facebook sending the personal data of 2.7 million European subscribers to Cambridge Analytica, large numbers of users have closed their accounts. Many have also closed their Twitter accounts to escape the permanent flow of tweets, which can be so disagreeable. The best examples of unplugging come from those who designed the new media, and who are, or have been, senior managers in the companies that develop or exploit them. They are well placed to appreciate their disadvantages and dangers.[292]

Putting the Place and Importance of the New Media into Perspective

Above all, it is necessary to put into perspective in one's mind the place and importance of the new media. One should realize that there is more to life than information and communication, and that these things should be instruments in the service of the content that precedes and follows them. The instruments are far less important than the content, which could be sent in a different way, deeper and more truthful, or which sometimes might better have not been sent at all.

They should also be set against former ways of working, of leisure and relationship, rediscovering the old ways if need be. One will then see that when the media are not absolutely necessary for the work in hand, they do not always improve efficiency or even speed, and that speed is rarely indispensable. It will be seen that the leisure activities proposed by the new media are not always more enriching or relaxing than traditional activities, and that the relationships formed through social networks are not deeper or more satisfying.

The pleasure, freedom, and depth of the reading of books will be rediscovered, along with newspapers and printed periodicals. The virtue of dead time, of silence, of solitude, of meditation, of contemplation, and of prayer will be ours again.

Standing Up to Social and Economic Pressure

One needs to stand back from all the social pressures that present the Internet, the smartphone, and the social networks in the most flattering light if one is to downgrade and restrain their use. Unconsciously they may be seen as fashion essentials and things to be imitated, which cannot be resisted. As we have seen, it should be realized that the development of the new media and their content are controlled by businesses that see the users as simple cogs in the profit machine.

It is important to shield oneself from all forms of exploitation. It is not enough to refrain from buying new versions of equipment, which is always being updated with new and useless gadgets. It is vital to avoid giving one's personal data to all those who seek to acquire and exploit it. For instance, by keeping one's private telephone number and email secret, many nuisance calls can be avoided from those commercial approaches and publicity stunts that can be so annoying.

Setting Filters

There are several filters that can be profitably used on mobile phones to limit calls and texts received to certain times or to restrict them to those coming from the contact list. Another filter connects every call to the voice mail, which allows the caller to be identified before the call is accepted. The latest fixed-line phones can be programmed not to ring when unidentified or undesirable callers try to make contact. Such calls have greatly increased in recent years as telephone marketing has progressed. There are also small devices, like Clibase, which also will block certain calls. And of course email providers allow certain messages to be automatically sent to the spam box. It is important to implement these things.

Unplugging

With all media, permanent connection should be systematically declined. It is essential that the television not always be on, even when one is engaged in other activities and just glances at it from time to time, hearing it in the background. This would seem to be obvious, but clearly is not for many households who pass the whole day to the sound and in sight of the television.

Going on the Internet, as one is often tempted to say, is also to be avoided. It means switching on the computer and randomly navigating the web. It should be eliminated at all costs if one wishes to be cured or to preserve one's health. Besides being tiring, such activity usually turns out to be of very little interest. There is also the risk of being more or less consciously driven in one's blind search by one's unhealthy passions.

Unplugging is clearly most important for the smartphone, perhaps through time filters, and for emails and text messages. Real-time alerts should be switched off. It is better to look at all the messages at a time of the day or week that is set aside for correspondence. If this is done, it becomes obvious that few messages need an instant reply, that many are soon irrelevant and need no reply, or that a single reply will cover several emails. Twitter's trap of instant reaction should be avoided. All this allows us to appreciate the value of distance and of taking time to reflect. Seeing the fleeting nature of news, we can just let it happen and avoid wasting time and energy.

Managing Online Time

In general online time should be managed so that it remains within set limits. If one cannot completely do without them, activities such as the television, the Internet, and social networks should be seen as secondary. Other personal activities should be given priority: homework for children, or meals and quality time spent together, which are not compatible with the media.

Television time should be limited, daily and weekly, to a fixed amount. The same should go for video games, web navigation, and social networks. Parents must watch carefully over their children in these matters and be ready to set strict limits to such activity. Seizing the phone when time is up is not recommended. It is better to agree to the rules in advance with the children and give them the responsibility of respecting them. This will gradually train them to handle such situations independently and more easily.

Managing Content

The best way of managing time spent online or in front of the television is to control the content, avoiding impulsive choices and random zapping. With the television, it is best to tune in to trustworthy channels and to select in advance quality programs. With the Internet, it is best to create a favorites list of the most useful and good quality sites so as to reach them at once as needed. This avoids much wasting of time and energy on irrelevancies.

The Virtue of Discretion

The new media encourage self-exposure in many ways, whether in public phone calls or on YouTube, Facebook, or other social networks. This, as we have seen, blurs the boundaries between public and private life, harming the intimacy and inner life of the person.

Those who use the new means of communication must re-learn the virtue of discretion as Pierre Zaoui[293] has recently emphasized. In today's society everything flows toward the public domain since everything is published. So, the virtues of intimacy and secret inner life must be rediscovered. It is these alone that allow the person truly to exist in the hidden mystery, which is his deepest nature.

Finding True Friendship Once More

Though at first excited by his numerous Facebook friends, *homo connecticus* will eventually realize that they're all fake. Friendship does not come at the click of a mouse and is not preserved in digital memory.

Rather than running after virtual friends and working to increase their number, it is better to rediscover the virtues of true friendship, which is not measured by numbers but by quality. It is gained and nourished through those long moments spent communing together, in touch at the deepest level; in other words, by practicing everything that the new media contradict with what is virtual, brief, and superficial.

Care for the Other in Composing the Message

With the new means of communication, we have seen how social bonds have lost much of their quality in the world of emails and text messages, poorly and hastily composed. It is important to take more care in their composition so as to give them once more the quality they deserve. This will show respect and human warmth for the receiver, especially in the introductory and concluding formulae that have been so debased compared to the correspondence of former times.

Taking Time

Many of the bad effects caused by the new media are linked, as we have seen, to the speed of use that they encourage. We have seen how, by saving time to make work more profitable, we lose time for the quality of personal life. As an antidote to the speed that governs the life of modern man, the Slow movement was started in the 1980s to promote slowness.[294] It is more vital than ever for *homo connecticus* to re-discover the benefits of slowness, which traditional societies have preserved. For in the speed of his communications and demands, he is the victim of hell. The everyday expression "Take your time" is full of wisdom. Time should not be poured out in an ungoverned stream at the behest of external factors. It should be devoted to one's own existence, which the person needs to be and to blossom in his inner life.

The Best Prevention: The Education of Children

Prevention is better than cure. By following the guidelines given above, the new media can be used in a limited way that prevents falling into an addiction from which it would be hard to escape. It is from childhood that one must learn to limit and control the use of the new media, and here the role of the parents is vital. Some of them take the radical path of total abstinence from the new media, often hoping thus to save their children. There is no television, computer, or tablet in the home. There is no smartphone elsewhere.

While this may be possible for small children, it cannot be applied completely when they grow older, unless one abstains from all forms of social life and all forms of technology as do the Amish in their closed and strongly religious community. Social pressure is very strong at school, as we have seen, and it is very difficult to escape from peer pressure in a community where almost everyone uses the new media. Furthermore, it is impossible to avoid using computers and the Internet, which are now part of the school curriculum from primary level.

The solution is to train children to manage the use of new media strictly that can only be done by closely supporting them right up to adolescence, which will be easier for them to handle if the main methods of self-control have been acquired in childhood. The parents must use their authority to grade the use of new media as a function of age, and must also teach their children to use them with reason in terms of space, time and content.

Serge Tisseron, the psychoanalyst, suggested the 3–6–9–12 rule for introducing children to the new media, but it is very lax. It allows tablets to be used from the age of 3; computers, television, and video games to be introduced between 3 and 6 years old; and telephone and the Internet between 9 and 12 years old.[295] One could suppose that he encourages a habit and creates an addiction at an age when acquired habits become firmly rooted in the mind for the whole life.

Before learning to use the new media, it is essential that children should learn to communicate using traditional methods so as to profit from their qualities and appreciate that they are not outdated or useless.

It is just as important for children to learn true sociability through real physical contact with other children of the same age before engaging in digital contact. They will thus easily see the richness of the one and the limits, poverty and partly illusory nature of the other. It is also important that they experience true comradeship and true, deep, and lasting friendship so as to appreciate their value as opposed to the fake friendships of Facebook.

In the same way, children should build up their own true personalities, assuming their defects as balance and progress require, and escape the temptation to create a virtual personality on Facebook that is bound to be disappointing since it is false.

They should be educated with traditional methods, handwriting on paper, mental arithmetic, and the use of printed dictionaries. This will help them to become disciplined in their work, to acquire and master such methods. They will learn the need for effort, and to take time for research, for organizing their knowledge, and for reflection. They must also learn ethical and spiritual values so as to be able to choose content with discernment.

Parents should ban the use of the new media in their children's bedrooms, especially the television and the smartphone so as to avoid their uncontrolled or lengthy use at night; for this brings certain problems, of which one is tiredness that undermines the next day's schoolwork. In the same context, total screen time should have a daily limit to stop it extending indefinitely. This can be combined with the use of DVDs and by recording programs of quality, whether educational or entertaining, which can be viewed later at a convenient time. The viewing time can be chosen so that it does not conflict with more important activities, and the choice of program can guide the taste of the children and accustom them to such programs. It has been shown that children who have the habit of watching certain kinds of program—for instance documentaries—will retain the habit into adulthood, provided, of course, that the content is adapted to their age.

It is important that parents do not allow their children to be carried away by the manifold suggestions and links of the Internet, but teach them to aim simply to fulfil their own needs, for information, for culture, or for their healthy hobbies. Many children discover violence and sex in their worst forms on the Internet, partly because their parents have not applied parental control but also because they have not been warned and given the personal training that would allow them to reject such content spontaneously. It is the same for the other dangers of the Internet, such as contact with strangers. However, parents should not simply choose content but also educate their children to look at content with a critical spirit and to use their own brains in deciding what to accept and what to reject.

Parents need to be present at several levels and give of their time. The addiction of children and adolescents to the television, to video games, or to the Internet may have several possible causes. However, it is often due, as we have already said, to parents who did not make enough effort to train and accompany their children. Worse, they may have used these things to keep their children quiet while they went about their own business. Parents have to take matters in hand from the start, and stay with their children until they have learnt enough to take matters in hand themselves, to use the new media with regard to the rules of place and time, to setting priorities and to abiding by cultural, moral, and spiritual values.

The Waldorf School of the Peninsula, in the heart of Silicon Valley, is rare in that it is not connected. Three quarters of the pupils are children whose parents work in the area, with Google, Apple, Yahoo, or Hewlett-Packard. These people who work to develop the digital economy and propagate it into every level of society are especially glad that in this school, their offspring are completely sheltered from computers, tablets, and smartphones right up till eighth grade.

Similar precautions are taken in the home to protect the children of the elite from what is fed to the common people. An article in the *New York Times* recently revealed that the CEOs of businesses in Silicon Valley prevented their children from using these different devices until they were fairly mature, and that even then, they were strictly controlled. The founder and CEO of Apple, Steve Jobs, was one such person as revealed by this article written by Steve Bilton. It was widely quoted in the international press and deserves to be quoted here at length to show his exemplary conduct:

> "So, your kids must love the iPad?" I asked Mr. Jobs […]. The company's first tablet was just hitting the shelves. "They haven't used it," he told me. "We limit how much technology our kids use at home."
>
> I'm sure I responded with a gasp and dumbfounded silence. I had imagined the Jobs's household was like a nerd's paradise: that the walls were giant touch screens, the dining table was made from tiles of iPads and that iPods were handed out to guests like chocolates on a pillow.
>
> Nope, Mr. Jobs told me, not even close.
>
> Since then, I've met a number of technology chief executives and venture capitalists who say similar things: they strictly limit their children's screen time, often banning all gadgets on school nights, and allocating ascetic time limits on weekends.
>
> I was perplexed by this parenting style. After all, most parents seem to take the opposite approach, letting their children bathe in the glow of tablets, smartphones and computers, day and night.
>
> Yet these tech C.E.O.'s seem to know something that the rest of us don't.
>
> Chris Anderson, the former editor of Wired and now chief executive of 3D Robotics, a drone maker, has instituted time limits and parental controls on every device in his home. "My kids accuse me and my wife of being fascists and overly concerned about tech, and they say that none of their friends have the same rules," he said of his five children, 6 to 17. "That's because we have seen the dangers of technology firsthand. I've seen it in myself; I don't want to see that happen to my kids."
>
> The dangers he is referring to include exposure to harmful content like pornography, bullying from other kids, and perhaps worse of all, becoming addicted to their devices, just like their parents.
>
> Alex Constantinople, the chief executive of the OutCast Agency, a tech-focused communications and marketing firm, said her

youngest son, who is 5, is never allowed to use gadgets during the week, and her older children, 10 to 13, are allowed only 30 minutes a day on school nights.

Evan Williams, a founder of Blogger, Twitter and Medium, and his wife, Sara Williams, said that in lieu of iPads, their two young boys have hundreds of books (yes, physical ones) that they can pick up and read anytime.

So how do tech moms and dads determine the proper boundary for their children? In general, it is set by age.

Children under 10 seem to be most susceptible to becoming addicted, so these parents draw the line at not allowing any gadgets during the week. On weekends, there are limits of 30 minutes to two hours on iPad and smartphone use. And 10- to 14-year-olds are allowed to use computers on school nights, but only for homework.

"We have a strict no screen time during the week rule for our kids," said Lesley Gold, founder and chief executive of the SutherlandGold Group, a tech media relations and analytics company. "But you have to make allowances as they get older and need a computer for school."

Some parents also forbid teenagers from using social networks, except for services like Snapchat, which deletes messages after they have been sent. This way they don't have to worry about saying something online that will haunt them later in life, one executive told me.

Although some non-tech parents I know give smartphones to children as young as 8, many who work in tech wait until their child is 14. While these teenagers can make calls and text, they are not given a data plan until 16. But there is one rule that is universal among the tech parents I polled.

"This is rule No. 1: There are no screens in the bedroom. Period. Ever," Mr. Anderson said. [...]

I never asked Mr. Jobs what his children did instead of using the gadgets he built, so I reached out to Walter Isaacson, the author of "Steve Jobs," who spent a lot of time at their home.

"Every evening Steve made a point of having dinner at the big long table in their kitchen, discussing books and history and a variety of things," he said. "No one ever pulled out an iPad or computer. The kids did not seem addicted at all to devices."[296]

The Silicon valley managers cited in the above article are not alone in setting limits to the new media for their families.

Tim Cook, who followed Steve Jobs as CEO of Apple, considers that the use of technology should be limited in schools and said that he, who has no child, didn't want his nephew to use a social network.[297] Bill Gates, founder and president of Microsoft, has revealed that he also limited his children's exposure to technology. His children asked for smartphones in their early adolescence but he and his wife, Melinda, ignored their complaints until they were 14. He sets rules to limit the use of digital devices in his home. For instance, he sets a time every evening after which all screens must be switched off.[298] Nir Eyal, a professor at Stanford Business School, an adviser to several companies, and author of *"Hooked: how to build a habit forming products,"* has described how he tries to protect his own family. He has a timer connected to the router in his home that switches off the Internet at a set time every day.[299] Chamath Palihapitiya, the former vice-president in charge of user growth at Facebook, said at a Stanford Business School event: "I don't use this shit and my kids are not allowed to use this shit either."[300]

Prevention of Undesirable Content, Abuse of Personal Data, Commercial Exploitation, and Propaganda

If we allow our children to use social networks or navigate the web within certain limits, we should protect them against the dangers that lie therein. They should be trained not to reveal on social media any personal data that could then be used against them to do them psychological harm. As we have seen, there is a veritable plague of mockery, humiliation, and bullying that can drive children and adolescents to depression or even suicide. Prudence is also needed in discussion forums that evil-minded sexual deviants may use to contact children and entice them into perverse and troubling relationships.

There are now many applications offered by service providers that allow parental control and can block access to content that could be dangerous or troubling for the young, for example, sexual, violent, or sectarian.

Adults also need to protect themselves from the different kinds of exploitation of their personal data that can cause all kinds of trouble. First of all, one should, as far as possible, avoid communicating personal data, be it details of oneself, one's postal address, email, or telephone number. On commercial sites where some data must be provided, the options that allow retransmission of this data or its use for marketing should be deselected.

The computer should be set to refuse cookies and to prevent the tracking of one's navigation. Search engines like DuckDuckGo can be used, or Firefox, with the private navigation option selected. In other search engines the option "do not track" can be selected, or applications that identify tracking sites and block them, like Ghost, can be used. Service providers use the autofill option insidiously to orient searches in the direction they desire. If it cannot be disconnected, its suggestions should be ignored, even though it will take longer to enter the search terms.

Spiritual Healing and Prevention

As we have seen, the negative effects of the new media are felt on the spiritual plane, and are caused by various spiritual factors. So, there is a need for spiritual prevention and healing.

Fasting from the New Media

Fasting is usually thought to be abstention from food, but the teaching of the Church Fathers shows that it has a much wider application. During the times of the fast, they encourage us to add to the fast of the mouth and the stomach a fast of all the senses, touch, sight, hearing, and touching. We should abstain from everything that gorges psychological life, alienating the spirit and enticing man away from the spiritual life that he needs.

In Orthodox countries it is traditional to abstain from worldly shows and concerts during Lent and to limit television time to a minimum. The aim of this is not deprivation, but to loose one's habitual bonds so as to be freer and readier for higher tasks, to turn from dispersion the better to attend to spiritual activities and the "one thing needful."

In this sense, fasting can be applied to the use of the new media. Their use is restricted and controlled with the aim of freeing oneself to regain openness to the spiritual healing of oneself and one's neighbor and to open oneself to God. The fast may be complete for periods, long or short, laid down in advance. Or it may simply involve restrictions on the type and duration of use: a strict selection of television programs and the limitation of Internet sites visited to those of some spiritual value.

Mastering Impulses, Desires, and Passions

Both spiritual healing and prevention imply a mastery of the impulses that drive us to use the new media at all times and everywhere. They require work to quench the desires and weaken the passions that go with them and impel us to using them for moral and spiritual harm. They should then become part of the whole ascetic life. In its widest sense, this is a struggle to eliminate the passions bit by bit and to develop the opposing virtues. For mankind, it is the best way of life.[301]

The Benefits of Humility

The new media, as we have seen, encourage generalized exhibitionism that takes root in the spiritual state of philautia (love of self). To oppose this, we must cultivate humility that dissolves the illusions and disappointments of vanity and pride. It truly builds us up in the love of God and our neighbor to which it gives first place.[302]

The Virtues of Silence and Solitude

We must rediscover as well the virtues of silence and solitude that the spiritual tradition of the Christian East combine in the notion of *hesychia*. This includes both outer silence and the inner calm to which it gives rise. The holy ascetics often reprove "vain words" or gossip, which they identify as a real passion. It is harmful as a waste of time and a distraction from more important occupations, but worse, it opens the door to other passions. Very often those long telephone conversations with unrestricted call plans and all those discussion forums on the Internet are nothing by a temptation to this passion.

By restricting conversations to the essential, by switching off the phone to provide long periods of silence, and by reserving times of solitude, modern man can rediscover himself. He can recover his inner life and re-forge himself in outer silence and inner peace. He can find once more the virtues of meditation, contemplation and prayer, and the riches of spiritual life, which his dispersion among worldly cares has denied him.

Making Time for Reading

It is important to take time to read the printed word, which has many advantages over reading on-screen.[303] In the context of spiritual life, reading has always been considered as essential. It not only serves to instruct, but also to nourish the soul with the grace of Holy Scripture and the charismatic experience of the saints.

Already in the third century Origen praised the merits of "godly reading" (*theia anagnôsis*), emphasizing however that it could only be fruitful when done steadfastly with attention and prayer.[304] Western monastic tradition codified the rhythm, length, and style of this practice at a very early date calling it *lectio divina*. After reading each section of the text, the reader next meditates on it to lead himself to contemplation.[305]

In the Eastern monastic tradition S.S. Pachomios and Basil included spiritual reading in their monastic rules with a freer form, yet considering it as completely indispensable for prayer. St John Cassian, another master of monastic life, also recommends it[306] while St John Chrysostom emphasizes that it is not restricted to monks, but that all the faithful who live in the world with families and professional cares also have great need of it.[307]

Without Fail Make Time for Prayer

As we have seen, the new media, especially the Internet, tend to take up time that should be used for prayer, even the time of monks. Those hermits who have become dependent often abbreviate drastically the divine services. Often smartphones remain switched on during the time of prayer, which they disturb with their ring tones. It is not uncommon to see the faithful, monks, or even the celebrants themselves look at their smartphones during divine services. They believe that they are justified by the need to be ready to serve their neighbor and the potential urgency of a call.

It is vital to have a strict rule in these matters and to stick to it. The time for prayer must be preserved absolutely inviolable. All those potentially disturbing connections must be switched off. It is also important not to engage in any work or conversation that cannot be finished by the time when prayer begins. If this is impossible, there must be the will to cut short at that time any ongoing activity.

Prayer can only be fruitful in silence, and so in solitude, in attention without outer or inner distraction, and in continuity for sufficient time without interruption. All these conditions are summed up by the term *hesychia*, which is at the heart of the spiritual path called hesychasm in Orthodox spiritual tradition. This was most precisely defined in the fourteenth century[308] but has its roots in the first centuries. This is shown by the texts collected from every age in the *Philokalia*,[309] an anthology that continually emphasizes as the foundations of spiritual life the notions of *nepsis* (vigilance and sobriety) and attention, which it sees as the conditions *sine qua non* of authentic prayer.

Caring for Neighbors

For Christianity, our relations with those close to us are extremely important. Christ taught that love for our neighbor is our most important duty, the most essential virtue after love for God. We have seen how the new media pretend to increase these relations in number, but in fact prevent them by imprisoning their users in isolation, or impoverish them by replacing the real with the virtual. Multifaceted relationships are replaced with one-dimensional links based on texts and images. Relationships are falsified through distorted presentations of oneself to others, qualities exaggerated, or identity hidden by pseudonyms. They may wither through the use of shortened messages lacking in any civility, or they may become superficial, deprived of attention through dispersion into *multitasking* of parallel activities and communication.

It is vital to build once more a true relationship with our neighbor, where each person is fully present with their full attention for the other, where there are the time and means needed to deepen it. Each person should attend in every way possible to the well-being of the other.

Paying Attention

As we have seen, the worst damage caused by the new media is to the faculty of attention, and consequently, to concentration. Their power to distract and disperse make attention more and more difficult, be it to one's own tasks, to others, or to God. Eastern Christian Tradition sees the spiritual life as needing the greatest attention, which it sees, with vigilance, as one of its two pillars. This very fact makes it a school of attention. Through vigilance (*nepsis*), which is basically a constant watching over oneself, and through attentive prayer, attention progressively develops, or is restored if it was formerly lost or distorted.

We must aim to reject permanently all temptations and even the most banal alien thoughts, not just thoughts themselves, but imaginings, memories, and desires. At the same time we should make an effort concentrate on the words of the prayer and to think of nothing else. Such is the way to strengthen attention so as to bring the mind and the soul to a state of stability, which nothing can disturb and to all our faculties a strength that no external power can weaken.

Notes

1. V.C. Strasburger, Professor of Pediatrics at the University of New Mexico notes: "The media represent some of the most under recognized and most potent influences on normal child and adolescent development in modern society. Because media influences are subtle, cumulative, and occur over a long period of time, parents, pediatricians, and educators may not be aware of their impact" ("Children, Adolescents and the Media," *Current Problems in Pediatric and Adolescent Health Care* 34, 2004: 54). M. Desmurget observes: "The causal link between the media and the symptoms they produce is often hidden by the time which elapses between exposure and the behavior it causes" (*TV Lobotomie. La vérité sciéntifique sur les effets de la télévision*, 2nd ed., Paris: J'ai Lu, 2013, 28).

2. *Contre le colonialisme numérique. Manifeste pour continuer à lire* (Paris: Albin Michel, 2013), 16.

3. See M. Hautefeuille and D. Velea, *Les addictions à l'Internet. De l'ennui à la dépendance* (Paris: Payot & Rivage, 2014), 165–187, which throws light on the responsibilities of business in cyber addiction and how they exploit it.

4. In the United States, which sets the standard, 80% of households possess at least three televisions, and more than 70% of children over eight have one in their bedroom.

5. Usually these are families with high moral, cultural or educational standards who are sufficiently well off to provide their children with various supervised activities.

6. There are of course different levels between total abstinence and complete saturation. Generally, viewing time is less amongst higher social classes, since they have the culture and the means to replace the television with alternative cultural and leisure activities. On the other hand, the lack of alternatives reinforces the place of the television.

7. See the work of L. Lurçat, quoted above.

8. See M. Desmurget, *TV Lobotomie. La vérité sciéntifique sur les effets de la télévision*, 2nd ed. (Paris: J'ai Lu, 2013), 54–58. N. Carr, *L' Internet, rend-t-il bête?* (Paris: Robert Laffont, 2011), 128–129. Studies have shown that the time spent in front of a computer screen increases the total time spent in front of screens in general. It does not replace television time except for the television time combined with the Internet

(cf. H. Dawley, "Time-wise, Internet Is Now TV's Equal," *Media-Life*, February 1, 2006.

9. A recent study has shown how frequently three media are used at once—television, computer or tablet and smartphone.

10. *Des enfances volées par la télévision. Le temps prisonnier*, 2nd ed. (Paris: François-Xavier de Guibert, 2004), 13, 29.

11. Ibid., 14. The author writes of the "violent" influence of the television for which he gives three reasons: "Firstly, the medium degrades reality, allowing all kinds of confusion and association by blurring the distinctions which are required for rational judgement. Secondly, the emotions are infected by the direct action of the images presented and their associated ambiance. Thirdly, there is a sophisticated manipulation of the viewer's desires and motives. This manipulation uses psychological techniques which encourage automatic imitation through their subliminal and subconscious action, and more or less conscious imitation through suggestion" (pp. 151–152). See also pp. 161–162 for the techniques of manipulation inherent in the television.

12. See L. Lurçat, *Des enfances volées par la télévision*, 37.

13. For an analysis of the different types of game see M. Hautefeuille and D. Velea, *Les addictions à internet. De l'ennui à la dépendance* (Paris: Payot & Rivage, 2014), 48–68.

14. The sentiment felt when confronted with new models and their owners of having an "old fashioned" phone, and the corresponding need to change it, encouraged by advertising, fashion, and peer pressure.

15. This is done by continuously creating new models, improved in flash memory, processor speed, data storage, image definition etc.; which make earlier models technically out of date, and unable to be used for the latest applications. In many cases, this obsolescence is deliberately built in to the devices to limit their useful lives.

16. Vance Packard saw clearly in 1960 in "The Waste Makers," David McKay co; Inc.; New York 1960, that the consumer society works according to this principle of double obsolescence, programmed by manufacturers and retailers.

17. The record is held by the singer, Katy Perry, who has 70 million followers.

18. See, for instance, *Epictète*, *Entretiens*, II, 5: "The materials are neutral, but the use we make of them is not."

19. See, for instance, Maximus the Confessor, *Centuries on Charity*, I, 40, 92; II, 73, 75, 76, 82; III, 1, 4; IV, 91.

20. This is the meaning that the psychoanalyst, Serge Tisseron has brought out in his work. See, for instance, 3-6-9-12; *Apprivoiser les écrans et grandir* (Toulouse: Editions Erès, 2013).

21. *Discours de la méthode*, 6th part.

22. *L'homme unidimensionelle* (Paris: Editions de minuit, 1966).

23. Ibid.

24. *La dimension cachée* (Paris: Edition du Seuil, 1971). See also: *Au delà de la Culture* (Paris: Edition du Seuil, 1979); *Le langage silencieux* (Paris: Edition du Seuil, 1984).

25. Marshall McLuhan, *Understanding the Media: The Extensions of Man* (Cambridge, MA: The MIT Press, 1994)
26. The title of Chapter 1.
27. McLuhan, *Understanding the Media*, 7. "The railway did not introduce movement or transportation or wheel or road into human society, but it accelerated and enlarged the scale of the previous human functions, creating totally new kinds of cities and new kinds of work and leisure," 8.
28. Ibid., 9.
29. He notes this (McLuhan, *Understanding the Media*, 18).
30. Ibid., 15.
31. Ibid., 20.
32. Ibid., 18.
33. Nicholas Carr, *The Shallows: What the Internet Is Doing to Our Brains* (New York: W. W. Norton & Company, 2010), 116.
34. Editions Gallimard, Paris, 1952, 25–28.
35. In the sense that Mircea Eliade gives to this expression that contrasts them to modern societies.
36. Tchouang-Tzeu, *nan-hoa-tchen-king,* Chapter 12K, in L. Wieger, *Les pères du système taoiste* (Paris: Edition Les Belles Lettres, 1950), 300–301 (translation modified).
37. *Pris dans la toile. L'esprit au temps du web* (Paris: Gallimard, 2012), 21–22.
38. This does not simply concern addicts (those who are dependent), but to a certain extent every user. As McLuhan writes: "By continuously embracing technologies, we relate ourselves to them as servomechanisms. That is why we must, to use them at all, serve these objects, these extensions of ourselves, as gods or minor religions." (McLuhan, *Understanding the Media*, 46). The religious character of the new media and their use has been strongly emphasized by Philippe Breton in his essay *Le Culte de l'Internet. Une menace pour le lien social?* (Paris: La Découverte et Syros, 2000). We will return to this point later.
39. Recently, a student at the University of Angers had his application for enrollment in a masters degree refused because he did not have a Twitter account.
40. Each appliance, from the printer to the refrigerator, the washing machine, and the coffee machine, is programmed to order automatically over the Internet any consumables it may need.
41. *L'Utopie de la communication. Le mythe du "village planétaire"* (Paris: La Découverte, 1997), 150–151.
42. *La Foule solitaire. Anatomie de la societé moderne* (Paris: Arthaud, 1964). Translation of *The Lonely Crowd: A Study of the Changing American Character* (Doubleday, 1950).
43. *Les enfances volées par la télévision. Le temps prisonnier*, 2nd ed. (Paris: François-Xavier de Guibert, 2004), 16.
44. *TV lobotomie. La vérité sciéntifique sur les effets de la télévision*, 51.
45. Up to 40 times an hour according to an American study. (K. Renaud, J. Ramsay and M. Hair, "You've Got Email!" Shall I Deal with It Now?" *International Journal of Human-Computer Interaction* 21 (2006), 313–322).

46. "Writing in the Age of Distraction," *Locus*, January 1999.

47. Carr, *The Shallows*, 131.

48. Cf ; *Essai sur les données immédiates de la conscience* (Paris: Alcan, 1889).

49. *TV lobotomie. La vérité sciéntifique sur les effets de la télévision*, 51.

50. Cf. *Physique*, IV, 10–11, 218b–219b.

51. J. Gleick, Faster. *The Acceleration of Just About Everything* (London: Abacus Press, 1999); C. Studeny, *L'Invention de la vitesse* (Paris: Gallimard, 1995); J.-M. Salmon, *Un monde à grande vitesse. Globalisation, mode d'emploi* (Paris: Seuil, 2000); J. Ollivro, *Quand la vitesse change le monde* (Rennes: Apogée, 2006); B. Warf, *Time-Space Compression. Historical Geographies* (London: Routledge, 2008); P. Josephe, *La Société immédiate* (Paris: Calmann-Lévy, 2008); R. Hassan, *Empires of Speed. Time and Acceleration of Politics and Society* (Leiden: Brill, 2009); H. Rosa and W.E. Scheuerman, *High Speed Society; Social Acceleration, Power and Modernity* (State College: Pennsylvania State University, 2009); H. Rosa, *Accélération. Une critique soclale du temps* (Paris: La Découverte, 2010); J.-L. Servan-Schreiber, *Trop vite; Pourquoi nous sommes prisonniers du court terme* (Paris: Albin Michel, 2010).

52. See J. Atali, *Histoire du temps* (Paris: Fayard, 1982).

53. This service offers next day delivery, but other sites offer same day delivery.

54. "Fatale liberté," in *Internet, l'inquiétante extase*, ed. A. Finkielkraut and P. Soriano (Paris: Mille et une nuits, 2001), 26.

55. Ibid., 48.

56. Cf. Aristotle, *Physics*, IV, 10–11; St Augustine, *Confessions*, XI, 14–28.

57. See, for example, J. Dumazedier, *Vers une civilisation de loisirs?* (Paris: Seuil, 1962).

58. Quoted by Carr, *The Shallows*, 140.

59. We will treat this point at length later.

60. *TV lobotomie. La vérité sciéntifique sur les effets de la télévision*, 120, with supporting scientific references.

61. This is an example of *task switching*, which is a form of *zapping*.

62. *TV lobotomie. La vérité sciéntifique sur les effets de la télévision*, 120, with a supporting scientific bibliography.

63. *Le Colonialisme N=numérique* (Paris: Albin Michel, 2013), 100.

64. *L'Utopie de la communication. Le mythe du "village planétaire"* (Paris: La Découverte, 1999), 5.

65. *Cybernétique et société* (Paris: Deux Rives, 1952).

66. P. Breton, *Le Culte de l'Internet. Une menace pour le lien social?* (Paris: La Découverte, 1999), 5.

67. *Cybernétique et societé*, 173.

68. One might object that today in the World identities are tending to become stronger, but this is simply a reaction to globalization.

69. Breton, *L'Utopie de la communication*, 5.

70. "L'ère de la facticité," in *technologies et symboliques de la communication*, ed. L. Sfez and G. Coutlee (Grenoble: Presses Universitaires de Grenoble, 1990), 39.

71. Pieces Et Main D'œuvre, *Le téléphone portable, gadget de destruction massive* (Montreuil: l'Echappée, 2008), 46.

72. One family out of two takes lunch in front of the television, and two out of three take dinner in front of it.

73. *L'Utopie de la communication*, 12, 160.

74. Ibid., 8.

75. *Le Culte de l'Internet. Une menace pour le lien social?*, 104.

76. *The Naked Sun* (New York: Doubleday, 1957). The action takes place on the planet Solaria. Its population is very small which allows each inhabitant to possess immense estates. The inhabitants are separated by large distances and are used to living alone. They are afraid of real concrete encounters and they almost never meet. They keep in touch through a holographic communication system, a prefiguration of our systems of virtual communication.

77. See J.Cl. Monod, *Ecrire à l'heure de toute message* (Paris: Flammarion, 2015), 66 *et passim*.

78. Cf. Breton, *L'Utopie de la communication*, 12, 153, 159.

79. Ibid., 153.

80. *La Machine Internet* (Paris: Editions Odile Jacob, 1999), 154.

81. Thuy Ong, "Sean Parker on Facebook: 'God Only Knows What It's Doing to Our Children's Brains,'" *The Verge*, November 9, 2017.

82. *La Machine Internet*, 161.

83. *Les addictions à Internet*, 205.

84. A good summary with well-developed arguments can be found in Michel Desmurget's book *TV lobotomie. La vérité scientifique sur les effets de la télévision*, 247–262 for the second point and pp. 273–318 for the first.

85. See ibid., 66.

86. "Policy Statement—Media Violence," *Pediatrics* 124 (2009): 1495.

87. *TV lobotomie. La vérité scientifique sur les effets de la télévision*, 318–319.

88. D. Kunkel, K. Eyal, K. Finnerty, E. Biely, and E. Donnerstein, *Sex on TV*, A Kaiser Family Foundation Report, November 2005, 21, 48, 51.

89. *TV lobotomie. La vérité scientifique sur les effets de la télévision,* 253.

90. "Adolescents, Sex and the Media: OOOOO, baby, baby-a Q & A," *Adolescent Medicine Clinics* 16 (2005): 273.

91. *TV lobotomie. La vérité scientifique sur les effets de la télévision,* 255.

92. A survey conducted in 2000 in America by the Television Company MSNBC.

93. According to the site Top Ten Reviews (Internet Filter Review, 2006).

94. *Online Victimization of Youth: Five Years Later* (National Center for Missing & Exploited Children Bulletin—#07-06-025, Alexandria, VA, 2006).

95. *Focus on the Family Poll*, October 1, 2003.

96. For these questions, see the excellent study by the psychiatrists Hautefeuille and Velea, *Les addictions à l'internet*, 101–111.

97. *The Economic Impact of Cybercrime and Cyberespionage*, Center for Strategic and International Studies, July 2013.

98. For example, the Internet brought the chemical GHB (gamma-hydroxybutyrate) to the notice of interested parties. Before that, it was known only to a few researchers. It is known as the rapist's drug, and the recipe for making it is online.

99. *Les addictions à l'internet*, 125.

100. For more on these questions see the work quoted above, Hautefeuille and Velea, *Les addictions à l'internet*, 127–134.

101. *Critique de la communication* (Paris: Seuil, 1992), 437.

102. On the way relationships between public and private life have developed, see his essay *La Condition humaine* (Paris: Calmann-Levy, 1961).

103. Translated from French computer application information.

104. *La Machine Internet.*

105. "*Fatale Liberté*," 19–20.

106. See M. Dugain and C. Labre, *L'Homme nu. La dictature invisible du numérique* (Paris: Robert Laffont and Plon, 2016), 52–58.

107. In 2015, at the request of the American security services, Yahoo developed software to search for precise data in the complete record of emails received by its users. Two former employees and a third person who was aware of the practice revealed that this service provider had searched several hundred million Yahoo Mail accounts at the request of the NSA or the FBI. Confronted with these revelations, the company replied that Yahoo respects the law and complies with the laws of the United States.

108. Metadata includes a great variety of information: the name of the sender of an email, the email address, the password and his IP address, the subject of the message, the email address of the destination, the date, the time and the time zone of the message, and the nature of the content and its format. For a social network the metadata include the user's name and geo-localization, the mobile phone used for a mobile phone connection and the date of the creation of the account. For the Internet it includes the search topics, the URLs accessed, the time of the visit, and the service provider.

109. In 2013 research showed that in a data base of 1.5 million people, four geographical locations were enough to identify 95% of the users. In 2007 researchers at the University of Columbia were able to identify the most senior management in Enron simply by looking at the number of emails sent and received and the average response time in a database containing 620,000 emails. By recording someone's metadata over the space of a week, researchers at the University of Ghent were able to reconstitute the life of the subject. An organization defending American civil liberties showed that it is even possible to predict where someone will be by analyzing data on the places frequented by the people he knows.

110. In his own inimitable way, the former French President, Nicolas Sarkozy stated (November 30, 2015): "When you look at the images of the jihadists, you are a jihadist."

111. A term that refers to the analysis of the behavior and profiles of customers.

112. *La Société du spectacle* (Paris: Buchet/Chastel, 1967).

113. See G. Bonnet, *La tyrannie du paraître* (Paris: Eyrolles, 2013).

114. See S. Tisseron, *L'Intimité surexposée* (Paris: Eyrolles, 2013).

115. *The Culture of Narcissism: American Life in an Age of Diminishing Expectations* (New York: W. W. Norton & Company, 1978).

116. *Le Culte de l'Internet*, 10–11. Reference to D. Le Breton, *L'Adieu au corps* (Paris: Metaillé, 1999).

117. *L'Adieu au corps.*

118. Ibid., 18.

119. D.A. Christakis and F.J. Zimmermann, "Media as a Public Health Issue," *Archives of Pediatrics and Adolescent Medicine* 160 (2006): 445.

120. *TV Lobotomie. La vérité scientifique sur les effets de la télévision,* 187–188.

121. See especially K. Windaele, G.N. Healy, D.W. Dunstan, A.G. Barnett, J. Salmon, J.E. Shaw, P.Z. Zimmett, and N. Owen, "Increased Cardiometabolic Risk Is Associated with Increased TV Viewing Time," *Medicine and Science in Sports and Exercise* 42 (2010): 1511–1518. The risk of death is increased by around 13% for an average exposure of 2–4 hours per day, and by 43% for an exposure of more than 4 hours per day.

122. *TV Lobotomie. La vérité scientifique sur les effets de la télévision*, 213. There is a long analysis of the links between obesity and the television on pages 190–213 of this book. It is well documented and supported by statistics.

123. The genetic factors that cause obesity are much less significant than overeating and lack of physical activity.

124. The links between obesity and the television, and the resulting problems, are well documented and analyzed statistically in M. Desmurget's book, *TV Lobotomie. La vérité scientifique sur les effets de la télévision*, 190–213.

125. *TV Lobotomie. La vérité scientifique sur les effets de la télévision*, 203–247.

126. Ibid., 214–229.

127. Research undertaken by J.R. Polansky and S. Glanz on 479 movies produced in the United States found around 2,700 scenes of tobacco smoking (*First-Run Smoking Presentations in US Movies 1999–2006*. Center for Tobacco Control, Research and Education, University of California, San Francisco, April 2007).

128. T.N. Robinson, H.L. Chen, and J.D. Killen, "Television and Music Video Exposure and Risk of Adolescent Alcohol Use," *Pediatrics* 102 (1998): 3.

129. L. Titus-Ernstoff, M.A. Dalton, A.M. Adachi-Medjia, M.R. Longacre, and M.L. Beach, "Longitudinal Study of Viewing Smoking in Movies and Initiation of Smoking by Children," *Pediatrics* 121 (2008): 15.

130. M.A. Dalton, J.D. Sargent, M.L. Beach, L. Titus-Ernstoff, J.J. Gibson, M.B. Ahrens, J.J. Tickle, and T.F. Healtherton, "Effect of Viewing Smoking in Movies on Adolescent Smoking Initiation: A Cohort Study," *Lancet* 362 (2003): 281.

131. *TV Lobotomie. La vérité scientifique sur les effets de la télévision,* 267.

132. Cf. *Pensées*, edition Bruschvicg, no. 82.

133. In 2015 there were 300 million active users of Instagram, the photo application of Facebook, who posted 70 million photos every day (*Le Monde*, April 10, 2015).

134. *La Société du Spectacle*, 3rd ed. (Paris: Gallimard, 1992), § 1.

135. A significant German word that means: "Vision of the World."

136. *La Société du Spectacle*, § 5.

137. Ibid., § 6.

138. Ibid., § 10.

139. Ibid., § 12.

140. Ibid., § 18.

141. Ibid., § 58.

142. The ghostly world of the television and its perverse effects on relations with reality were analyzed and criticized in a radical way as early as 1956 by G. Anders, *L'Obsolescence de l'homme, Vol. 1, Sur l'âme à l'époque de la deuxième revolution industrielle*, trad. Fr. (Paris: Ivréa, 2002), 117–241.

143. *Des enfants volés par la television* (Paris: François-Xavier de Guibert, 2004), 135.

144. Ibid., 134–135, 147.

145. Ibid., 148.

146. Gallimard, Paris, 2001.

147. *Des enfants volés par la television*, 58 and 54–55.

148. Ibid., 59.

149. William Gibson, *Neuromancer* (New York: Berkley Publishing Group, 1994), 51.

150. *Critique de la communication*, 17: "Tautism: neologism created by contracting 'Tautology' (The idea that since I repeat something I prove it which is present in all media), and 'Autism' (the communication system makes us deaf and dumb, isolated from others and quasi autistic.)." This neologism suggests a totalitarian aim. Cf. pp. 110–111.

151. *Les Simulacres et la simulation* (Paris: Galilée, 1981).

152. Ibid.

153. Ibid.

154. The best known are Google Glass from Google, Holo Lens from Microsoft, and Oculus Rift from Facebook.

155. Oxford University Press, Oxford, 1964.

156. See D. Leloup and M. Tual, "Une photo de Mark Zuckerberg ravive la peur de la réalité virtuelle," *Le MondI*, February 22, 2016. "Matrix" refers to the film *"Matrix."*

157. *La République* [The Republic], VII, 514a–516c [translated—AT].

158. Anxiety is a diffuse complaint whose source is not immediately obvious; fear, however, has an immediate and recognizable cause.

159. The new media, and especially the television, have a great responsibility for this feeling. They recount, often most dramatically, the smallest accident or the slightest aggression occurring in the global village, thus giving a false impression of intensity and proximity.

160. Hautefeuille and Velea, *Les addictions de l'Internet*, 95.

161. Cf. C. Martin, *Représentation des usages du téléphone portable chez les jeunes adolescents*, Xth Colloque bilatéral franco-roumain. CIFSIC Université de Bucarest, June 28–July 3, 2003.

162. The person is considered less as a being in relation—something emphasized to excess by modern personalism—than as a being who is distinguished from others of the same kind or the same nature by incommunicable characteristics that make of him a unique and irreplaceable being.

163. See Hautefeuille and Velea, *Les addictions de l'Internet*, 156–163.

164. *Pensées*, ed. Bruschvicg, no. 139.

165. Breton, *L'Utopie de la communication*, 12, 50.

166. *Internet, rend-il bête?* (Paris: Robbert Laffont, 2010), 301–303.

167. M.H. Immordino-Yang, A. McColl, H. Damasio, and A. Damasio, "Neural Correlates of Admiration and Compassion," *Proceedings of the National Academy of Sciences of the United States of America* 106 (2009): 8021–8026, especially p. 8024.

168. See extracts of an interview with M.H. Immordino-Yang, "Rapid-fire Media May Confuse your Moral Compass, Study Suggests," *Science Daily*, April 14, 2009.

169. *Pensées*, ed. Bruschvicg, no. 147.

170. Christopher Lasch, *The Culture of Narcissism: American Life in an Age of Diminishing Expectations* (New York: W. W. Norton & Company, 1979), 50.

171. Maggie Jackson, *Distracted: The Erosion of Attention and the Coming Dark Age* (Amherst, NY: Prometheus Books, 2008), 79.

172. Carr, *The Shallows*, 133.

173. Among the recent accounts of depression provoked by intense use of the new media, see G. Birenbaum, Vous m'avez manqué. Histoire d'une dépression française (Paris: Les Arènes, 2015).

174. Tisseron, *Apprivoise les écrans et grandir*, 13. See also Hautefeuille and Velea, *Les addictions à l'Internet*, 40. These two psychiatrists observe that as a consequence, "addiction is a solution before becoming a problem" (ibid., 146, 232) and quote several examples that show "how part of the internet serves to compensate a dissatisfaction or a difficulty which is often a problem in real life" (p. 149).

175. D. Smahel, E. Helsper, L. Green, V. Kalmus, L. Blinka, and K. Olafsson, *Excessive Internet Use Among European Children?* EU Lids Online, November 2012, 5.

176. Hautefeuille and Velea, *Les addictions à l'Internet*, 45. We refer to this work for a precise analysis of the different kinds of cyber-dependence—to video games (pp. 48–64), to role play games online (pp. 64–68), to chats (pp. 68–84), to social networks (pp. 85–86), to news (pp. 86–93), to blogs (pp. 93–95), to tablets and smartphones (pp. 95–96)—and to different kinds of cyber-assisted addiction—to chats (pp. 98–100), to sex (pp. 101–112), and to purchases (pp. 139–143).

177. Ibid., 43–44.

178. *L'Utopie de la communication*, 55.

179. There have been several in-depth investigations, particularly on the effects of the television, see especially those of T. Macbeth Williams, *The Impact of Television: A Natural Experiment in Three Communities* (London: Academic Press, 1986); M. Winn, *The Plug-in Drug: Television, Computers, and Family Life* (London: Penguin Books, 2002); L. Lurçat, *Des enfances volées par la télévision. Le temps prisonnier*, 3rd ed. (Paris: François-Xavier de Guibert, 2004; Desmurget, *TV Lobotomie* (especially pp. 41, 121–132, 133–134, 144–146, 147); there is a vast supporting bibliography in this work.

180. Cf. Desmurget, *TV Lobotomie*, 134, referring to E.A. Vandewater et al., "Time Well Spent? Relating Television Use to Children's Free Time Activities," *Pediatrics* 117 (2006): 181–191.

181. Desmurget, *TV Lobotomie*, 173, 175.

182. These studies, and others, are quoted by Desmurget, *TV Lobotomie*, 144–147.

183. It might be said that both television and Internet require a certain amount of attention, and that video games require far more. But neuroscience distinguishes two distinct systems of attention. Each depends on different neuron circuits. One is stimulated in an automatic exogenous manner, and the other in a voluntary endogenous manner. Exposure to audiovisual effects stimulates the first that can then develop so much as to stifle the second.(Cf. Desmurget, *TV Lobotomie*, 147, where the supporting bibliography may be found.)

184. See Desmurget, *TV Lobotomie*, 129.

185. *Homo videns. Televisione e post-pensiero* (Rome and Bari: Laterza, 1998).

186. "L'immagine ha distrutto la cultura occidentale," interviewed by Leonetta Bentivoglio in *La Republica* du 15 juillet 2011, 6.

187. Contents of the Petit Robert and the Grand Robert, respectively.

188. For comparison, a lexicological study of the works of Guy de Maupassant showed that he used 18,256 words, more than Zola or Prouost, but less than Flaubert (see T. Selva, "Une étude quantitative du vocabulaire de Maupassant," *L'Angélus. Bulletin de l'Association des Amis de Guy de Maupassant* 12 (2001–2002): 41–48).

189. See, for example, A. Lieury, S. Lorant et F. Champault, "Loisirs numériques et performances cognitives et scolaires : une étude chez 27 000 élèves de la 3ᵉ des collèges," *Bulletin de psychologie* 530 (2014): 99–125.

190. *L'Utopie de la communication. Le mythe du "village planétaire,"* La Découverte, Paris, 1997, 142–143.

191. For example, in French: à demain = a2m1 ; à lundi = al1di ; à plus tard = a+ ; bien sûr = b1sur ; bonsoir : bsr ; impossible : 1posibl ; je le savais = jle sav ; qu'est-ce que c'est ? = keskeC ; quoi de neuf ? = koi29 ; vraiment : vrMen.

192. For example: aussi vite que possible = asap (de l'anglais "as soon as possible") ; bon après-midi = bap.

193. For example: ça y est = ayé ; comment ça va ? = komensava ; d'accord = dak ; en tout cas = entouK ; j'espère que tu vas bien : jSpR ktu va bi1 ; laisse tomber = l'StonB ; pourquoi = pk.

194. "L'immagine ha distrutto la cultura occidentale," interviewed by Leonetta Bentivoglio in *La Republica* du 15 juillet 2011, 6.

195. See Carr, *The Shallows*, 126–131.

196. See Desmurget, *TV Lobotomie*, 134–141.

197. See Lurçat, *Des enfances volées par la télévision*, 48.

198. *Homo videns. Televisione e post-pensiero.*

199. "F-Shaped Pattern for Reading Web Content," *Nielsen Norman Group*, April 17, 2006.

200. H. Weinreich, H. Obendorf, E. Herder, et M. Mayer, "Not Quite the Average: An Empirical Study of Web Use," *ACM Transaction on the Web* 2, no. 1 (February 2008).

201. "How Little Do Users Read?," *Nielsen Norman Group*, May 6, 2008.

202. "Puzzling Web Habits Across the Globe," *ClickTale Academy Blog*, 31 July 2008.

203. See the paper by Z. Liu, "Reading Behaviour in the Digital Environment," *Journal of Documentation* 61 (2005): 700–712.

204. Cf. Carr, *The Shallows*, 138.

205. Carr, *The Shallows*, 122.

206. Ibid., 176.

207. *Discourse on Thinking* (New York: Harper & Row, 1966), 56.

208. Cf. Hautefeuille and Véléa, *Les addictions à Internet*, 89.

209. *Les Simulacres et la simulation*, 119.

210. Desmurget, *TV Lobotomie*, 117.

211. For a description of the difference between information and learning, the following work may be consulted: D. de Rougemont, "Information n'est pas savoir," *Diogène* 116 (1981): 3–19.

212. PLATO, *Phaedrus,* gutenberg.org/ebooks/1636 (*Phèdre*, 274–275.)

213. Peter Suderman, "Your Brain Is an Index," *The American Scene. An Ongoing Review of Politics and Culture*, May 11, 2009.

214. Ibid.

215. See, for example, St. Augustine, *Confessions*, Books X and XI.

216. *Talks to Teachers on Psychology* (New York: Henry Holt and Company, 1916), 143. This is the conclusion of Chapter 12 (pp. 116–143), which demonstrates this point.

217. *Instructional Design in Technical Areas* (ACER Press, 1999), 4.

218. This analysis of Sweller's work and its relation to the use of the Internet is taken from Carr, *The Shallows*, 125.

219. *Pris dans la Toile. L'esprit au temps du Web*, 25.

220. As regards the dispersive nature of multitasking and its deplorable effects on attention, see especially R. Casati, *Contre le colonialisme numérique* (Paris: Albin Michel, 2013), 99–100.

221. See E. Ophir, C. Nass et A.D. Wagner, "Cognitive Control in Media Multitaskers," *Proceedings of the National Academy of Sciences* 106, no. 37 (2009): 15583–15587.

222. A clear correlation has been demonstrated between the time passed in front of the television during childhood and attention deficits in adolescence. See C.E. Landhuis, R. Poulton, D. Welch, R.J. Hancox, "Does Childhood Television Viewing Lead to Attention Problems in Adolescence? Results from a Prospective Longitudinal Study," *Pediatrics* 120 (2007): 532–537.

223. See Desmurget, *TV Lobotomie*, 87–89.

224. Carr, *The Shallows*, 118.

225. M. Richtel, "As Doctors Use More Devices, Potential for Distraction Grows," *New York Times* du 14 décembre 2011, Voir aussi P. Buscell, "Do Electronic Devices in Health Care Present New Risks for Patient Safety?," *Plexus Institute*, 15 décembre 2011; R. Buckwalter-Poza, "Treat, Don't Tweet : The Dangerous Rise of Social Media in the Operating Room," *Pacific Standard. Politics & Law, Business & Economics, Health & Behavior, Nature & Technology*, 16 avril 2014.

226. P.J. Papadakos, "Electronic Distraction : An Unmeasured Variable in Modern Medicine," *Anesthesiology News* 37 (November 2011).

227. Cf. N. Carr, *Internet rend-il bête ?* (*The Shallows*) (Paris: Robert Laffont, 2010), 26.

228. Ibid., 39–63.

229. Ibid., 54, 51–52, 57.

230. Carr, *The Shallows*, 48.

231. Ibid., 116.

232. M. Merzenich, quoted by Carr, *The Shallows*, 120.

233. Carr, *The Shallows*, 120.

234. *L'Utopie de la communication*.

235. *Le Culte de l'Internet*.

236. *Histoire de l'utopie planétaire. De la cité prophétique à la société globale* (Paris: La Découverte, 1999).

237. *La Tyrannie de la communication* (Paris: Gallimard, 2004), 37–38.

238. *L'Adieu au corps*.

239. *Vitesse virtuelle. La cyberculture aujourd'hui* (Paris: Abbeville, 1997).

240. *Critique des réseaux* (Paris: PUF, 2003).

241. *Le Culte de l'Internet*, 76–83.

242. Carr, *Internet rend-il bête ?* (*The Shallows*), 211–247. He is writing of the religious dimension of Google rather than "The Church of Google," an organization recently founded in Canada, and recognized by the State. It believes that Google is a god and venerates it for the following divine qualities that it is thought to possess: (1) Google is all-knowing. (2) Google is everywhere present. (3) Google replies to every prayer (that is to say, every request typed in to the search bar) (4) Google could be immortal. (5) Google is infinite. (6) Google remembers everyone. (7) Google can do no evil and does not wish it. (8) Google is more beloved and sought after than any other god. (9) Google is the only god whose existence is proved.

243. Houghton Mifflin, Boston, 1950.

244. *L'Utopie de la communication*, 15–37, 49–58.

245. *Éditions Odile Jacob*, Paris, 2000.

246. A rich bibliography can be found on these two movements in the article by N. Le Dévédec and F. Guis, "L'humain augmenté, un enjeu social," *SociologieS*, October 19, 2013.

247. See my article "La divinisation comme projet et modèle chrétien du perfectionnement et de l'augmentation de l'homme," in Marc Feix and Karsten Lehmkühler (éd.), *Homme perfectible, homme augmenté*, hors-série de la *Revue d'éthique et de théologie morale*, 286, 2015, pp. 181–197.

248. According to recent statistics (2015), 78% of French people connect before going to sleep and 75% on awaking.

249. A.B. Downey, "Religious Affiliation, Education and Internet Use," arXiv:1403.5534, March 24, 2014.

250. Recall that psychoanalysis has had its greatest impact in protestant countries where confession did not exist.

251. M. Béra and E. Mechouan write that "The internet is a permanent outlet which absorbs the urges of those who connect to chat under the most absurd identities. The participation of the 'tribe' provides 'amateur' psychonalysis and assuages the instincts. What's more, an army of confidants act as a psychological safety valve which helps to calm down the stress accumulated during the day. [...] There is no lack of analysts (in the psychoanalytic sense of the word) ready to plunge down the road opened by Sherry Turkle who pioneered 'follow me on line.' Therapy itself is achieved through confession. This allows us to see the Protestant character of the Internet compared to the Catholic way" (*La Machine Internet*, 154–155).

252. See the section entitled "Confession et anticonfession" in *La Culture du narcicissime* (Paris: Flammarion, 2008), 45–50.

253. See my book *La Vie sacramentelle* (Paris: Cerf, 2004), 11–12. See also P. Patrick O'Grady, "Réalité virtuelle et réalité de la vertu : l'éthique des relations basées sur Internet," communication au Premier colloque international sur les médias numériques et la pastorale orthodoxe, Athens, May 7–9, 2015.

254. Finkielkraut et Soriano, *Internet, l'inquiétante extase*, 44.

255. Article in the International Colloquium "Les nouveaux médias et la pastorale orthodoxe," Athens, May 7–9, 2015.

256. See my article in the International Colloquium "Orthodox Theology and the Sciences," Université Saint-Clément d'Ohrid, Sofia, April 26–29, 2011 : "Patristic Views on the Nature and Status of Scientific Knowledge."

257. "Social Media : Is It a Positive or Negative for a Person's Spiritual Journey ? An In-depth Analysis," *Peterpilt*, March 25, 2013.

258. See, for instance, J. Rice, *The Church of Facebook: How the Hyperconnected Are Redifining Community* (Colorado Springs: David C. Cook, 2009).

259. The way the new media substitute a virtual community for a concrete community is described by B.J. Kallenberg, *God and Gadgets : Following Jesus in a Technological Age* (Eugene: Cascade Books, 2011).

260. For a precise description of these passions see my book *Thérapeutique des maladies spirituelles*, 6th ed. (Paris: Cerf, 2013).

261. For a precise analysis see Desmurget, *TV Lobotomie*, 247–262.

262. See ibid., 34–35, 273–305.

263. See ibid., 289–305.

264. See ibid., 305–317.

265. See I. Hausherr, *Philautie, de la tendresse pour soi à la charité selon saint Maxime le Confesseur*, Rome, 1952, and my *Thérapeutique des maladies spirituelles*, 151–157.

266. On this subject, see my book *Thérapeutique des maladies mentales*, 2nd ed. (Paris: Cerf, 2007), 101–132.

267. *The Culture of Narcissism.*

268. See M.B. Crawford, *The World Beyond Your Head: On Becoming an Individual in an Age of Distraction* (New York: Farrar, Straus & Giroux, 2015).

269. Translated as "original" in the Western Tradition.

270. See, for instance, Maxime le Confesseur, *Questions à Thalassios* [Questions to Thalassios], Introduction, SC 529, pp. 135–139 ; Basile de Césarée, *Lettres*, II, 2 ; Calliste et Ignace Xanthopouloi, *Centurie*, 23.

271. Maxime le Confesseur, *Questions à Thalassios* [Questions to Thalassios], 137 [translated—AT].

272. See, among others, Macaire d'Égypte, *Homélies (coll. III)*, XXV, 5, 4.

273. Cf. Macaire d'Égypte, *Homélies (coll. II)*, IV, 4; Isaac le Syrien, *Discours ascétiques*, 68.

274. Cf. Calliste et Ignace Xanthopouloi, *Centurie*, 19, 23, 24, 25.

275. Macaire d'Égypte, *Homélies (coll. II)*, XXXI, 6.

276. Cf. NicÉtas StÉthatos, *Centuries*, III, 2 ; 6 ; 19.

277. Macaire d'Égypte, *Homélies (coll. II)*, VI, 3.

278. *Mystagogie* [Mystygogy], XXIII, PG 91, 697C [translated—AT]

279. *Sur la garde de l'intellect*, dans *Philocalie des Pères neptiques*, trad. fr., vol. 2, Abbaye de Bellefontaine, Bégrolles-en-Mauges, 1980, p. 67.

280. *Trois centuries, pratique, physique et gnostique*, III, 18, dans *Philocalie des Pères neptiques*, trad. fr., vol. 4, Abbaye de Bellefontaine, Bégrolles-en-Mauges, 1982, p. 127.

281. In *Philocalie des Pères neptiques*, trad. fr., vol. 10, Abbaye de Bellefontaine, Bégrolles-en-Mauges, 1990, pp. 39–53.

282. Ibid., vol. 3, 1981, 15–82.

283. In I. Hausherr, *La Méthode d'oraison hésychaste*, Rome, 1927, 54–76.

284. "Certain of the saints have called attention 'guarding the spirit,' others 'guarding the heart,' others 'sobriety,' others '*hesychia*' and others have given it different names. But all these names refer to one and the same thing" (In *Philocalie des Pères neptiques*, trad. fr., vol. 10, Abbaye de Bellefontaine, Bégrolles-en-Mauges, 1990, p. 50).

285. See, for instance, K.S. Young, "Internet Addiction: Symptoms, Evaluation and Treatment," in *Innovations in Clinical Practice: A Source Book*, ed. L. VandeCreek and T. Jackson, vol. 17 (1999), 19–31 ; Id., "CBTIA : The First Treatment Model for Internet Addiction," *Journal of Cognitive Psychotherapy : An International Quarterly* 25 (2011): 304–312. Y. Khazaal, C. Xirossavidou, R. Khan, Y. Edel, F. Zebouni, and D. Zullino, "Cognitive Behavioral Treatments for 'Internet Addiction,'" *The Open Addiction Journal* 5 (2012): 30–35; Hautefeuille and Véléa, *Les addictions à Internet*; Dr A.-M. Sergerie, "Cyberdépendance. La dépendance aux médias sociaux et à la technologie mobile," *Psychologie Québec* 31 (2014): 41–43.

286. For example, at Daxing to the south of Beijing there is a specialized center that has admitted over 6,000 young people since 2006, all addicted to video games (see "La désintox à marche forcée," *Le Courrier international*, n° 1261 (January 1–7, 2015): 31.

287. The self-discipline applied to drive off the new media or to limit their use is promoted in the United States as *self-binding*.

288. See, for example, D. Roberts, "My Life Offline," article in *Outside Magazine* translated in *Le Courrier international* n° 1261 of the January 7, 2015, pp. 26–28, 30.

289. See C.N. Cep, "L'abstinence numérique, un nouveau credo," article du *New Yorker* traduit dans *Le Courrier international* n° 1261 du January 7, 2015, p. 32.

290. Fitness and beauty centers usually based on hydrotherapy and various applications of thermal spas.

291. See C. Rollot, "Digital Detox, le jeûne des hyperconnectés," *Le Monde*, March 10, 2015.

292. Justin Rosenstein, the inventor of Facebook "likes," modified the operating system of his portable computer to block Reddit, removed Snapchat, which he compares to heroin and set limits to his use of Facebook. In August, this 34-year-old technical director took stronger measures to restrain his use of social media and other addictive technologies. After purchasing a new iPhone, he asked his assistant to implement parental control to prevent him from downloading applications. One of Rosenstein's colleagues, Leah Pearlman, a former product manager at Facebook, installed a plug-in on her web navigator to eliminate her Facebook news flow, and hired a social media manager to monitor her Facebook page so that she doesn't have to. Nir Eyal, author of "Hooked: how to build a habit forming products," revealed that he uses an extension of Chrome called DF YouTube, "which scrubs out a lot of those external triggers" and recommends an application called Pocket Points, which "rewards you for staying off your phone when you need to focus." Lauren Brichter, who designed the "pull to refresh" mechanism used to update Twitter flows, and adopted by other applications, has blocked certain websites, turned off push notifications, restricted his use of the Telegram app to message only with his wife and two close friends, and tried to wean himself off Twitter. He charges his phone in the kitchen, plugging it in at 7pm and not touching it until the next morning (P. Lewis, "Our Minds Can Be Hijacked: The Tech Insiders Who Fear a Smartphone Dystopia," *The Guardian*, October 6, 2017.

293. *La Discrétion, ou l'art de disparaître* (Paris: Autrement, 2013).

294. See the popular book of Carl Honoré, *Éloge de la lenteur* (Paris: Marabout, 2005).

295. *3-6-9-12. Apprivoiser les écrans et grandir*.

296. Nick Bilton, "Steve Jobs Was a Low-Tech Parent," *The New York Times*, September 10, 2014.

297. S. Gibbs, "Apple's Tim Cook: 'I Don't Want My Nephew on a Social Network,'" *The Guardian*, January 19, 2018.

298. A. Sulleyman, "Bill Gates Limits His Children's Use of Technology," *The Independent*, April 21, 2017.

299. Lewis, "Our Minds Can Be Hijacked."

300. H. Koslowska, "Former Facebook Executive Has Sworn Off Social Media Because He Doesn't Want to Be 'Programmed,'" *Quartz*, December 11, 2017.

301. Elsewhere I have described at length the passions as sicknesses of the soul and the virtues as symptoms of well-being. I have explained how patristic tradition sees the conversion of the one into the other in terms of a methodical spiritual therapy (*Thérapeutique des maladies spirituelles*). The reader may consult this work for further details.

302. On the manifestations, the meaning and the benefits of humility see ibid., 677–709.

303. See the long analysis and proofs provided by Simone, *Pris dans la toile*, and Casati, *Contre le colonialisme numérique*.

304. *Lettre à Grégoire le Thaumaturge.*

305. Cf. Guigues II le Chartreux, *L'Échelle des moines.*

306. *Conférences*, XIV, 11.

307. *Commentaire sur saint Matthieu*, II, 5.

308. See J. Meyendorff, *Grégoire Palamas et la mystique orthodoxe* (Paris: Seuil, 2002).

309. *Philocalie des Pères neptiques*, 7 vol., Abbaye de Bellefontaine, Bégrolles-en-Mauge, 2004. A selection of these texts with special reference to prayer is presented by J. Gouillard in *Petite philocalie de la prière du cœur* (Paris: Seuil, 1979).

Index

Tisseron, Serge, 163, 174 n.20
Toffler, Alvin, 37
tradition-directed man, 22
transhumanism, 140, 144
transparency, 98, 99
  culture of, 64
  ill effects of, 98–9
tweets (mini-messages), 10, 26, 39, 43, 44,
    66, 91, 97, 99–101, 118, 124, 130, 146,
    150, 158
Twitter, 10, 35–6, 73, 83, 149, 158
typing errors, 31
Tzeu-Koung, 16

unity, notions of, 153
university systems, new media's role in, 20

vanity, pride and, 148–9, 169
Véléa, Dan, 92, 94–5, 107
videoconferencing, 24
video games, 6–7, 56, 105
video sharing, 10
vigilance, 170, 171
  notions of, 153

violence, sex and
  Internet, 56–8
  television, 54–6
  video games, 56
virtual friends, 161
virtual reality, 84–7
  application of allegory of cave, 88–9
  artificial, 88
  and augmented reality, 88
  navigating, 76
  pride of place for image, 81–4
visual signals, 150

Weiner, Norbert, 37–8
Wiener, Norbert, 137–9, 145
Wijnbeerg, Rob, 71
Williams, Evan, 166
Williams, Sara, 166
World Transhumanist Association, 140

YouTube, 10, 148–9, 161, 178 n.107

Zaoui, Pierre, 161
Zuckerberg, Mark, 88